FORWARD

The TWO MOORS WAY will ever be a reminder that
walk the 2,700 miles of rural footpaths with ┐

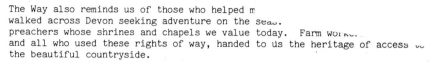

The Way also reminds us of those who helped m
walked across Devon seeking adventure on the sea⌐.
preachers whose shrines and chapels we value today. Farm woⲓⲕⲩ⌐
and all who used these rights of way, handed to us the heritage of access ∽
the beautiful countryside.

Devon is fortunate in having two National Parks within its boundaries, yet
few explore beyond the crowded tourist areas. The Two Moors Way leads those
who seek true recreation into the quiet, beautiful, but almost unknown
hinterland of Devon. To the small villages of stone, cob and thatch. To
high hills and secluded wood and valleys. To the real Devon.

The Way is open to all because of those who care for the countryside and our
footpaths, especially the Ramblers' Association.

Whether you walk all or only part of the Way, you will find what has united
us in our determination to keep what we have enjoyed for generations - a
pleasant, peaceful countryside that gives us full opportunity to live our
lives and earn our way with contentment.

T.PINNEY

Chairman, Amenities and Countryside Committee,
Devon County Council.
1976

IMPORTANT INFORMATION

SIGNING-IN BOOK FOR WALKERS COMPLETING THE TWO MOORS WAY
North: Exmoor National Park Information Centre, Lynmouth.
South: The Information Centre at Ivybridge Leisure Centre.

Open moorland of Dartmoor and Exmoor is NOT signposted
or waymarked. Not only is marking alien to the wild landscape, but it destroys your experience of being in a
wilderness. The walker may roam freely on Dartmoor
Access Land - tinted lilac on the relevant maps.

A Grid North is on every map page to help when taking a
compass bearing.

The Mid-Devon section of the Way has been upgraded to
the same standard as the Heritage Coast Path, with
signposts, waymarked posts and many good bridges, thanks
to the Countryside Commission and Mid-Devon District
Council.

J.R.Turner
Hon.Sec.T.M.W.Committee
1993

Hangershell Rock

Some Ancient WAYMARKERS

Hamel Down Cross

Hobajohn's Cross

Bennett's Cross

Huntingdon Cross

GENERAL INTRODUCTION

The TWO MOORS WAY runs between Ivybridge in South Devon and Lynmouth on the North Devon coast. It is approximately 163 km (102 miles) long if the route is strictly followed, but in some places there are bad or good weather alternatives and it is unlikely that you will be able to resist diversions to visit places of interest near-by. So be prepared for a somewhat longer walk, take it slowly and enjoy yourself.

The terrain is very varied, with stretches of open moor, deep wooded river valleys, green lanes and muddy fieldpaths and also some unavoidable lengths of road. It is hoped in future to open up new rights of way to reduce the latter, but much will depend on the way in which you treat the privilege of passing through the farmlands. A gate left open for an animal to stray, a broken bottle to cut its feet or a plastic bag to choke it, may lose the goodwill of a farmer for ever. This is not a tourist route and bins for your litter are not provided. Please take it with you so that the way will not be marred for others by unsightly debris of your picnicing.

A list of accommodation known to welcome Ramblers is given in a separate leaflet. This is up-dated from time to time. The most recent leaflet can be obtained by sending a stamped addressed envelope to the address given on the back cover.

Much of the route is hilly, so the distances you plan to walk must take this into account. Though an active Rambler may be able to complete the transit over a week-end, the majority will need much longer, even a full fortnight, if the richness of the countryside, its antiquities, churches and many other scheduled buildings and its panoramic views are to be appreciated.

Dartmoor has more antiquities than any other National Park in Britain and there are Prehistoric remains on Exmoor also. Much use was made of granite in the 15th - 17th Centuries. It is found on farms as well as churches and great houses as door and window frames, troughs and grind-stones. Roughcast rubble and cob are also common. The latter, much in evidence in Mid-Devon, consists of a mix of stiff clay compacted with chopped straw and seems to have been known in Devon since the 13th Century though the art of building with this material died about 1850. Usually the thicker the wall the older the building. On average cob walls are about 3ft thick, though sometimes they are as much as 4ft 6in. Raw cob is sandy to reddish brown but both it and roughcast or plastered rubble are often colour-washed as protection from the weather. Cob deteriorates rapidly if rain gets in from the top, so even walls which are not parts of buildings have slate or thatch coping. When cob goes down to ground level there is often a tarred strip along the bottom. In older houses, brick is seldom used except for chimney stacks.

The native woodlands are mainly oak or beech, but coniferous plantations have encroached the landscape in places. Though not intrinsically ugly, they offend the Devon purist. Fortunately elm was never a dominant tree, so that the depredations of Dutch elm disease are not conspicuous.

The typical Devon hedge has a core of stones, built up with turf so that it very soon appears as a solid bank on top of which grow shrubs and even full-sized trees. In many places hedges have been removed in recent years to make the fields larger and ease the handling of machinery, but there is now some doubt if this is wise because of erosion, which wire or wooden fencing does nothing to impede. Hedges often reduce the view but they provide a wealth of interesting wayside flowers and wild life.

Do not expect to find the footpaths easy going. Many of them are muddy. The open moor is also liable to be wet. Boots are essential. Walking shoes, however stout, are really not suitable.

Before you start out, read through the overview notes for the sections of the route. These will tell you the type of country to expect and give some guidance about access to the area. You will also find brief notes referring to the features you will pass on the individual maps. These are not exhaustive and you will probably wish to read more in specific books and guides obtainable locally at places of interest.

The route follows recognised highways, open moor and public rights of way. Some alterations to the route have been agreed since the Two Moors Way was opened in 1976. These are shown, but some changes are still under consideration. If such are made, they will be clearly signposted and way-marked.

The scale of the maps is approximately 1 : 18,000. Grid references in the margins enable the walker to relate his position to the appropriate parts of Ordnance Survey Maps. The Tourist maps of Dartmoor and Exmoor cover the area through which the way passes and relate the route to the surrounding countryside. The 1 km intervals can be used to estimate the distances, (1km = 5/8 mile). There is no key for identification of footpaths, green lanes and roads, but solid lines show hedges, walls or fences while dashes indicate open roads, tracks or footpaths. Dotted lines are used when open moor may be crossed without definitive path. Access areas on Dartmoor are coloured lilac.

The maps are numbered. The North-bound traveller should read straight through the book, while the South-bound should read the overview and then turn to the back and read forwards. Specific verbal instructions are only given to clarify points where confusion can arise.

OVERVIEW OF THE ROUTE

IVYBRIDGE

Ivybridge is a fast growing town on the B 3213 (old A 38). It has a number
of small light industries such as the mill which makes high quality paper,
but a large proportion of the inhabitants commute to Plymouth, Torbay and
the South Hams. There is a good bus service from Exeter, Plymouth and Torbay
with connections to long distance services. The trains of the Western Region
no longer stop at Ivybridge and the nearest railway station is at Plymouth.
Most of the through road traffic uses the fast dual carriage-way A 38 which
makes hitch hiking to the starting point of the Two Moors Way difficult.

IVYBRIDGE - SCORRITON   Maps N 1-5 : S 30-34   Distance 19 km
After leaving Ivybridge the route is entirely across uninhabited open moorland, with virtually no shelter. The walker must be prepared for sudden
changes in the weather, with mist, heavy rain and cold winds even in Summer.
Protective clothing, food and a compass are essential.
This section of the Way is scattered with Bronze Age remains in the form of
hut circles and enclosures, cairns, kists and stone rows such as are described
in Worth's 'Dartmoor'. There are remains of tin mining activity on Erme
Plains and in the Huntingdon Warren area and disused china clay workings a
short distance from the route at Redlake. The track of the Redlake tramway
is a good guide when crossing Ugborough Moor in poor visibility. The Abbot's
Way is less easy to identify and is followed only briefly.

SCORRITON - JORDAN   Maps N 6/7 : S 28/29   Distance 11 km
This is a very hilly section of the route, crossing the valleys of the
Holy Brook and Dart and climbing up onto the moor to cross Sherberton
Common before dropping into the valley of the West Webburn. New Bridge,
a narrow mediaeval structure, carries the B 3357 from Princetown via Dartmeet
to Ashburton. For those who wish to tackle the Two Moors Way in sections this
is a good place to leave or join the route. With the exception of Holne, the
villages in this area are little more than hamlets.

JORDAN - MARINERS' WAY   Maps N 8-10 : S 25-27   Distance 16 km
Travellers wishing to use the Bellever Youth Hostel should leave the route
by turning west at Jordan Mill or at the next cross-roads to the north.
Widecombe-in-the-Moor is worth a visit and the route can be rejoined without
any retracing of steps by by-passing a piece of open moor. Much of this
section of the route is over open moor where protective clothing, food and
a compass may be needed. In this case, however, there are roads quite close
to either side of the track. The B 3212, which is crossed about 1 km north
of the Warren House Inn, is the main road across Dartmoor from Plymouth or
Tavistock to Exeter via Moretonhampstead. There is a bus service only on
Summer week-ends.

THE MARINERS' WAY   Map N 11 : S 24   Distance 4 km
Between Yardworthy and Teigncombe the Two Moors Way uses a short section
of the Mariners' Way which once led from Dartmouth to Bideford, but of which
only part of the Dartmoor stretch can be identified.

TEIGNCOMBE - DREWSTEIGNTON   Maps N 11-13 : S 22-24   Distance 10 km
The greater part of this section of the route lies in the valley of the River
Teign. It is necessary to follow lanes as far as Chagford Bridge, but the
rest of the way is by paths beside the River Teign or at higher level below
Castle Drogo, with a short stretch of high undulating ground near Drewsteignton
village. There is a bus service from Okehampton to Bovey Tracey via Chagford
and Moretonhampstead. The A 382, crossed near Dogmarsh bridge, is the main
road from Okehampton to Bovey Tracey.

DREWSTEIGNTON - MORCHARD BISHOP Maps N 13-18 : S 17-22   Distance 24 km
The A 30, 1.7 km north of Drewsteignton, marks the boundary of the Dartmoor
National Park. Thus the greater part of this section of the route is in the
Mid-Devon area.
Undulating agricultural land is networked with narrow lanes and footpaths.
Devon County Council has cleared ancient rights of way and way-marked them.
To avoid annoyance to farmers, keep to the official paths and observe the
countryside code at all times. The northward way has some easting. The route
crosses the A 30, A 3072 and A 377 roads and also the Exeter-Okehampton and
Exeter-Barnstaple branch railway lines. The former line is closed to passenger
trains, but the latter is still open with a station at Morchard Road. There is
a reasonable bus service on the A 30 between Okehampton and Exeter and also on
the A 377 from Crediton to Barnstaple, so that there is access by public
transport to this section of the Two Moors Way.

MORCHARD BISHOP - HAWKRIDGE   Maps N 18-26 : S 9-17   Distance 36 km
The route passes through farming country, with Dartmoor and Exmoor visible
on the horizons of somewhat featureless views. While keeping in the main to
high ground, it dips into a number of valleys to cross small rivers which
drain westwards into the Taw.
Witheridge and Knowstone are the only places of any size along the Way. The
former, on the B 3137, has buses to Tiverton. There are also buses between
Taunton and Barnstaple on the new A 361 (North Devon Link road). Extreme care
must be taken when crossing this fast road.
The boundary of the Exmoor National Park runs just north of West Anstey, while
the Dane's Brook at Slade divides Somerset from Devon. North of this boundary
the bye-laws permitted the running of bulls with cows in fields which are
crossed by public footpaths long before the practice became legal elsewhere.
As always the walker is advised to avoid close contact with mixed herds and to
keep dogs well under control wherever there are animals about.

HAWKRIDGE - WITHYPOOL   Maps N 26/27 : S 8/9   Distance 11 km
The preferred route follows the River Barle, keeping to its east bank through
a beautiful wooded valley but, after exceptionally wet weather, Tarr Steps
may be flooded and impassable and the alternative, somewhat shorter route,
over Parsonage Down and the shoulder of Withypool Hill should be used.
From the Dulverton road just out of Withypool there is a footpath to the
Exford Youth Hostel. This is shown as route E5 on page 8 of the Exmoor
National Park booklet - 'Waymarked Walks 2'.

WITHYPOOL - HOAR OAK   Maps N 27-32 : S 3-8   Distance 19 km
The Way keeps mainly to high ground with dips to cross and recross the River
Barle. It is for the most part uninhabited, though it crosses the B 3358
north-east of Cornham Farm and skirts to the west of Simonsbath. Protective
clothing, food and a compass should be carried. From Exe Head northwards
there are views over the Bristol Channel.

HOAR OAK - LYNMOUTH   Maps N 32-34 : S 1-3   Distance 10 km
The Way runs approximately north/south over open moor of Cheriton Ridge, with
wide views on either side. It then follows a lane to Scoresdown. Near
Smallcombe Bridge it enters a waymarked permissive path through Combe Park,
National Trust property, to Combe Park Lodge near Hillsford Bridge. It crosses
the A 39, then climbs to follow the spectacular high level path along the
Cleaves above the East Lyn River. The final descent to Lynmouth is very steep.

LYNMOUTH
Lynmouth, at the northern end of the Two Moors Way, is virtually one town with
Lynton. The houses cluster on the steep sides of the East and West Lyn Rivers
and along the coastal strip. The area is very popular with summer visitors
and has holiday accommodation and other services as well as a Youth Hostel at
Lynbridge, a short distance up the valley of the West Lyn and an Exmoor
National Park Information Centre. The nearest rail service is Minehead, but
buses run along the Somerset and North Devon coast.

                         ORDNANCE SURVEY MAPS

    The following maps may prove useful as an overview of the route :
    Tourist map of Dartmoor (1:63360 i.e. 1.57cm to 1km or 1in to 1 mile)
    Tourist map of Exmoor   (1:63360   "   "   )
    Leisure Map of Dartmoor (1:25 000 i.e.4cm to 1km or 2½in to 1 mile)

TO AND FROM THE TWO MOORS WAY

Car owners are advised to park, take public transport to the far end of the Way and walk back. It is essential to use buses at both ends of the route, but the central section can be travelled by train. The recommended connections are Lynmouth - Barnstaple - Exeter - Plymouth - Ivybridge, but it is also possible to go via Minehead. Morchard Road, half way along the Way is on the Exeter - Barnstaple branch line.

Since deregulation it is impossible to give a list of companies which may be operating buses, but details of long distance services can be obtained from

> National Travel, Ltd
> Victoria Coach Station,
> Buckingham Palace Road,
> LONDON, SW1W 9TP
> Telephone 071-730-0202

or

> National Express,
> Bristol Enquiry Centre
> Telephone 072-671121

Local services from Plymouth, Exeter or Torbay to Ivybridge are run by Western National which has an enquiry office at :

> Bretonside Bus Station
> PLYMOUTH, PL4 OJP
> Telephone 0752-222666

Services to Lynton/Lynmouth from Bude and Barnstaple as well as Exeter, Tiverton, Tiverton Parkway and Minehead are run by Devon General which has an enquiry office at :

> Paris Street Bus Station,
> EXETER, EX1 2JP
> Telephone 0392-56231

Besides buses to the two ends of the Two Moors Way, a number of roads which intersect the route carry services, but these are infrequent, subject to changes from year to year and sometimes seasonal. It is important for the walker to check before setting out.

Full details of local services in Devon are available from Devon Transport Co-ordination Centre, Telephone 0392-382800.

Quickbeam Tin Workings
and Viaduct for Redlake
China Clay Pipe Line

RELICS OF
THE TIN
INDUSTRY

Ruined Tinners' Hut ~
Erme Pound

Mortar Stone

Stone with broken Mould,
polished Axle Socket and
Slot for Stamp Frame~
Hook lake

Mould Stone ~reused
in wall near Dockwell

Ruin of Blowing House - used as Chapel by Rev. Keeble Martin

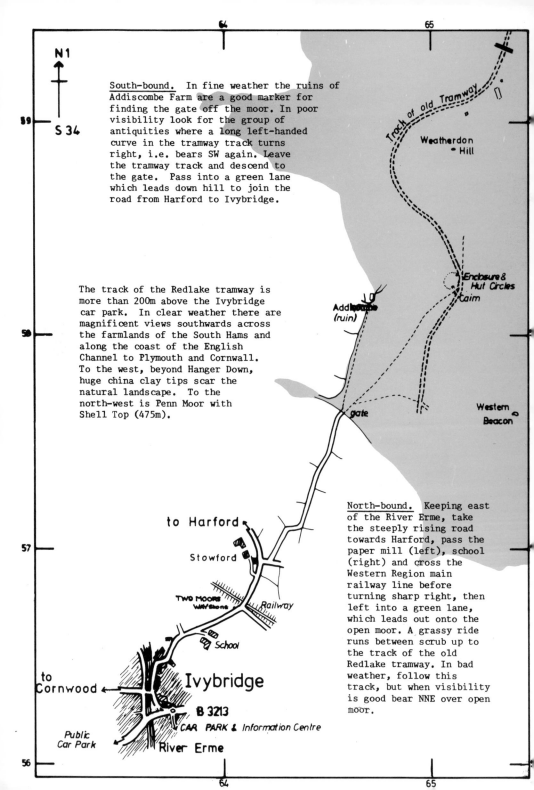

N 1

S 34

64

65

59

58

57

56

South-bound. In fine weather the ruins of Addiscombe Farm are a good marker for finding the gate off the moor. In poor visibility look for the group of antiquities where a long left-handed curve in the tramway track turns right, i.e. bears SW again. Leave the tramway track and descend to the gate. Pass into a green lane which leads down hill to join the road from Harford to Ivybridge.

The track of the Redlake tramway is more than 200m above the Ivybridge car park. In clear weather there are magnificent views southwards across the farmlands of the South Hams and along the coast of the English Channel to Plymouth and Cornwall. To the west, beyond Hanger Down, huge china clay tips scar the natural landscape. To the north-west is Penn Moor with Shell Top (475m).

Track of old Tramway

Weatherdon Hill

Enclosure & Hut Circles

Cairn

Addiscombe (ruin)

Western Beacon

gate

to Harford

Stowford

TWO MOORS WAY Stone

Railway

School

Ivybridge

to Cornwood

B 3213

CAR PARK & Information Centre

Public Car Park

River Erme

North-bound. Keeping east of the River Erme, take the steeply rising road towards Harford, pass the paper mill (left), school (right) and cross the Western Region main railway line before turning sharp right, then left into a green lane, which leads out onto the open moor. A grassy ride runs between scrub up to the track of the old Redlake tramway. In bad weather, follow this track, but when visibility is good bear NNE over open moor.

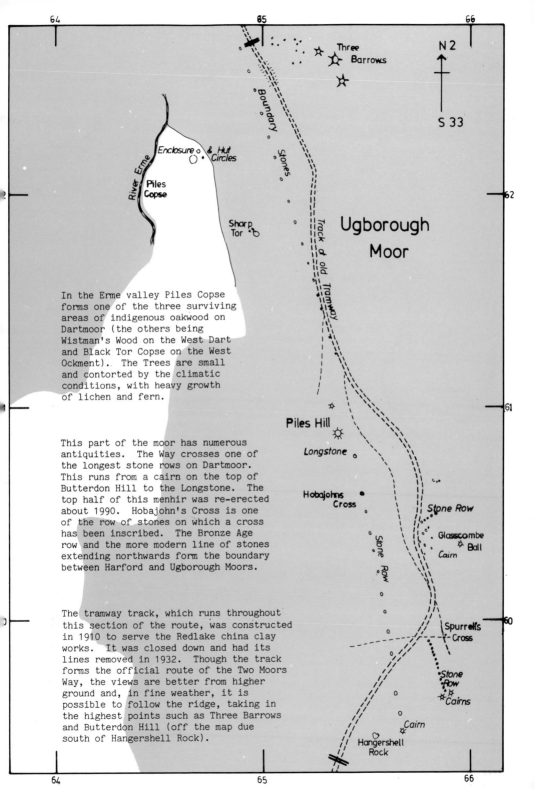

64 65 66

N 2

S 33

Three Barrows

Boundary Stones

River Erme

Enclosure & Hut Circles

Piles Copse

Track of old Tramway

Ugborough Moor

Sharp Tor

62

In the Erme valley Piles Copse forms one of the three surviving areas of indigenous oakwood on Dartmoor (the others being Wistman's Wood on the West Dart and Black Tor Copse on the West Ockment). The Trees are small and contorted by the climatic conditions, with heavy growth of lichen and fern.

61

Piles Hill

Longstone

This part of the moor has numerous antiquities. The Way crosses one of the longest stone rows on Dartmoor. This runs from a cairn on the top of Butterdon Hill to the Longstone. The top half of this menhir was re-erected about 1990. Hobajohn's Cross is one of the row of stones on which a cross has been inscribed. The Bronze Age row and the more modern line of stones extending northwards form the boundary between Harford and Ugborough Moors.

Hobajohns Cross

Stone Row

Glasscombe Ball

Cairn

Stone Row

The tramway track, which runs throughout this section of the route, was constructed in 1910 to serve the Redlake china clay works. It was closed down and had its lines removed in 1932. Though the track forms the official route of the Two Moors Way, the views are better from higher ground and, in fine weather, it is possible to follow the ridge, taking in the highest points such as Three Barrows and Butterdon Hill (off the map due south of Hangershell Rock).

Spurrells Cross

60

Stone Row

Cairns

Cairn

Hangershell Rock

64 65 66

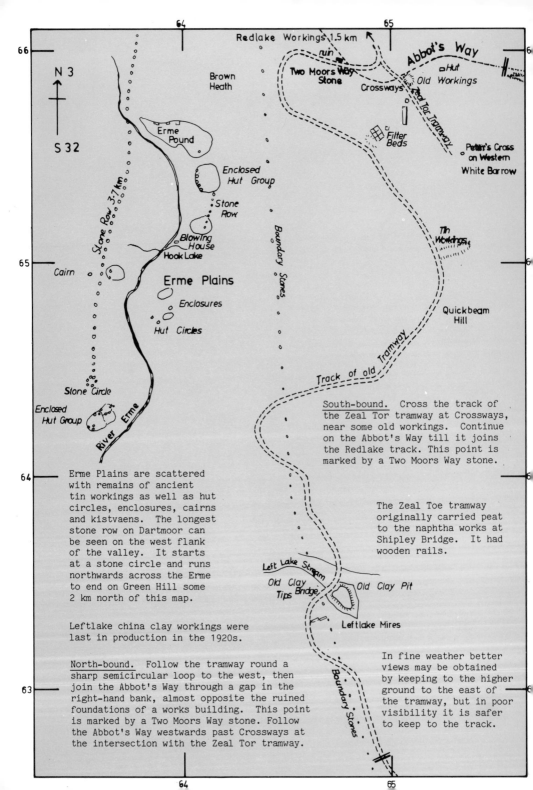

N 3

S 32

Redlake Workings 1.5 km

Abbot's Way

Brown Heath

Two Moors Way Stone

Crossways

Old Workings

Hut

Zeal Tor Tramway

Erme Pound

Filter Beds

Petre's Cross on Western White Barrow

Enclosed Hut Group

Stone Row 3.7 km

Stone Row

Blowing House

Hook Lake

Cairn

Tin Workings

Erme Plains

Boundary Stones

Enclosures

Hut Circles

Quickbeam Hill

Stone Circle

Track of old Tramway

Enclosed Hut Group

River Erme

South-bound. Cross the track of the Zeal Tor tramway at Crossways, near some old workings. Continue on the Abbot's Way till it joins the Redlake track. This point is marked by a Two Moors Way stone.

Erme Plains are scattered with remains of ancient tin workings as well as hut circles, enclosures, cairns and kistvaens. The longest stone row on Dartmoor can be seen on the west flank of the valley. It starts at a stone circle and runs northwards across the Erme to end on Green Hill some 2 km north of this map.

The Zeal Toe tramway originally carried peat to the naphtha works at Shipley Bridge. It had wooden rails.

Left Lake Stream

Old Clay Tips

Bridge

Old Clay Pit

Leftlake Mires

Leftlake china clay workings were last in production in the 1920s.

Boundary Stones

North-bound. Follow the tramway round a sharp semicircular loop to the west, then join the Abbot's Way through a gap in the right-hand bank, almost opposite the ruined foundations of a works building. This point is marked by a Two Moors Way stone. Follow the Abbot's Way westwards past Crossways at the intersection with the Zeal Tor tramway.

In fine weather better views may be obtained by keeping to the higher ground to the east of the tramway, but in poor visibility it is safer to keep to the track.

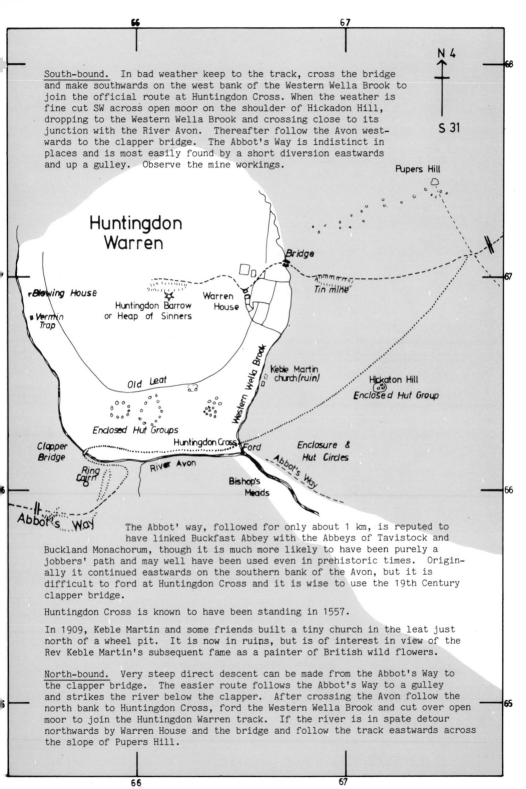

N 4

↑

S 31

South-bound. In bad weather keep to the track, cross the bridge
and make southwards on the west bank of the Western Wella Brook to
join the official route at Huntingdon Cross. When the weather is
fine cut SW across open moor on the shoulder of Hickadon Hill,
dropping to the Western Wella Brook and crossing close to its
junction with the River Avon. Thereafter follow the Avon westwards to the clapper bridge. The Abbot's Way is indistinct in
places and is most easily found by a short diversion eastwards
and up a gulley. Observe the mine workings.

Pupers Hill

Huntingdon
Warren

Bridge

Blowing House

Tin mine

Vermin
Trap

Huntingdon Barrow
or Heap of Sinners

Warren
House

Keble Martin
church (ruin)

Hickaton Hill
Enclosed Hut Group

Old Leat

Western Wella Brook

Enclosed Hut Groups

Huntingdon Cross

Ford

Enclosure &
Hut Circles

Clapper
Bridge

Ring
Cairn

River Avon

Abbot's Way

Bishop's
Meads

Abbot's Way

The Abbot' way, followed for only about 1 km, is reputed to
have linked Buckfast Abbey with the Abbeys of Tavistock and
Buckland Monachorum, though it is much more likely to have been purely a
jobbers' path and may well have been used even in prehistoric times. Originally it continued eastwards on the southern bank of the Avon, but it is
difficult to ford at Huntingdon Cross and it is wise to use the 19th Century
clapper bridge.

Huntingdon Cross is known to have been standing in 1557.

In 1909, Keble Martin and some friends built a tiny church in the leat just
north of a wheel pit. It is now in ruins, but is of interest in view of the
Rev Keble Martin's subsequent fame as a painter of British wild flowers.

North-bound. Very steep direct descent can be made from the Abbot's Way to
the clapper bridge. The easier route follows the Abbot's Way to a gulley
and strikes the river below the clapper. After crossing the Avon follow the
north bank to Huntingdon Cross, ford the Western Wella Brook and cut over open
moor to join the Huntingdon Warren track. If the river is in spate detour
northwards by Warren House and the bridge and follow the track eastwards across
the slope of Pupers Hill.

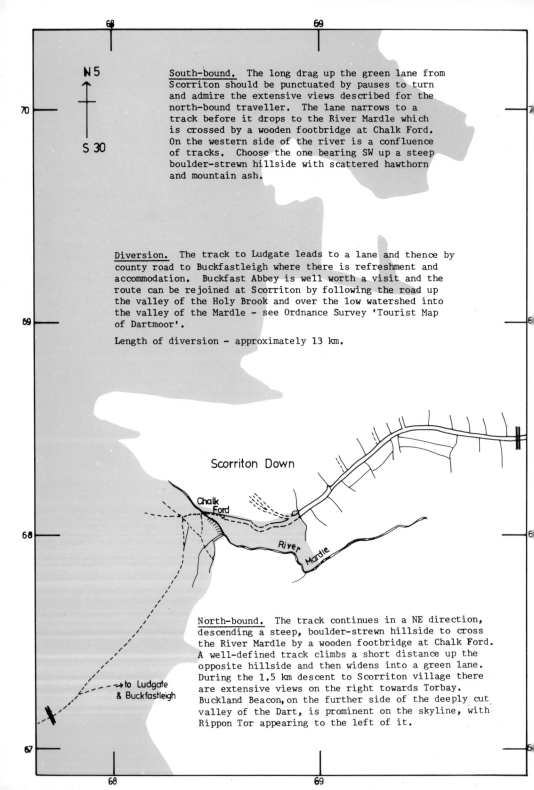

South-bound. The long drag up the green lane from Scorriton should be punctuated by pauses to turn and admire the extensive views described for the north-bound traveller. The lane narrows to a track before it drops to the River Mardle which is crossed by a wooden footbridge at Chalk Ford. On the western side of the river is a confluence of tracks. Choose the one bearing SW up a steep boulder-strewn hillside with scattered hawthorn and mountain ash.

Diversion. The track to Ludgate leads to a lane and thence by county road to Buckfastleigh where there is refreshment and accommodation. Buckfast Abbey is well worth a visit and the route can be rejoined at Scorriton by following the road up the valley of the Holy Brook and over the low watershed into the valley of the Mardle - see Ordnance Survey 'Tourist Map of Dartmoor'.

Length of diversion - approximately 13 km.

N 5
S 30

Scorriton Down

Chalk Ford

River Mardle

to Ludgate
& Buckfastleigh

North-bound. The track continues in a NE direction, descending a steep, boulder-strewn hillside to cross the River Mardle by a wooden footbridge at Chalk Ford. A well-defined track climbs a short distance up the opposite hillside and then widens into a green lane. During the 1.5 km descent to Scorriton village there are extensive views on the right towards Torbay. Buckland Beacon, on the further side of the deeply cut valley of the Dart, is prominent on the skyline, with Rippon Tor appearing to the left of it.

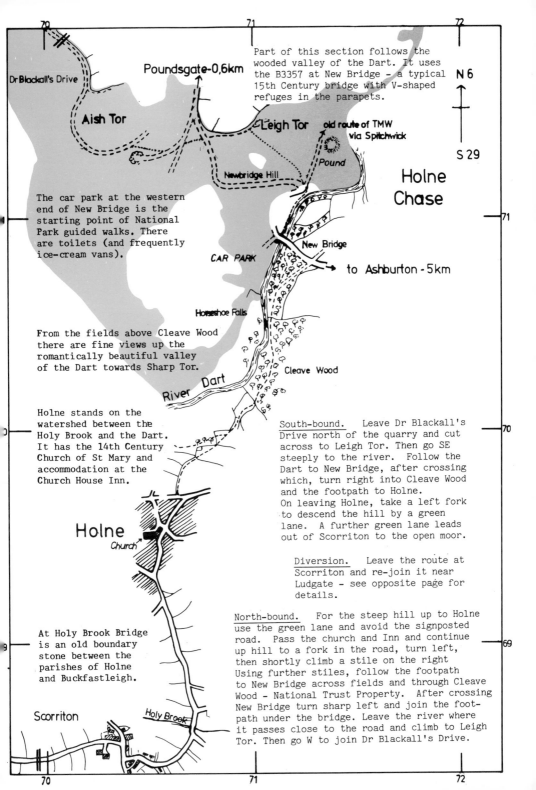

Part of this section follows the wooded valley of the Dart. It uses the B3357 at New Bridge – a typical 15th Century bridge with V-shaped refuges in the parapets.

N 6

S 29

Poundsgate-0,6km

Dr Blackall's Drive

Aish Tor

Leigh Tor

old route of TMW via Spitchwick

Pound

Newbridge Hill

Holne Chase

The car park at the western end of New Bridge is the starting point of National Park guided walks. There are toilets (and frequently ice-cream vans).

CAR PARK

New Bridge

to Ashburton - 5km

Horseshoe Falls

From the fields above Cleave Wood there are fine views up the romantically beautiful valley of the Dart towards Sharp Tor.

Cleave Wood

River Dart

Holne stands on the watershed between the Holy Brook and the Dart. It has the 14th Century Church of St Mary and accommodation at the Church House Inn.

South-bound. Leave Dr Blackall's Drive north of the quarry and cut across to Leigh Tor. Then go SE steeply to the river. Follow the Dart to New Bridge, after crossing which, turn right into Cleave Wood and the footpath to Holne. On leaving Holne, take a left fork to descend the hill by a green lane. A further green lane leads out of Scorriton to the open moor.

Holne

Church

Diversion. Leave the route at Scorriton and re-join it near Ludgate - see opposite page for details.

North-bound. For the steep hill up to Holne use the green lane and avoid the signposted road. Pass the church and Inn and continue up hill to a fork in the road, turn left, then shortly climb a stile on the right Using further stiles, follow the footpath to New Bridge across fields and through Cleave Wood - National Trust Property. After crossing New Bridge turn sharp left and join the footpath under the bridge. Leave the river where it passes close to the road and climb to Leigh Tor. Then go W to join Dr Blackall's Drive.

At Holy Brook Bridge is an old boundary stone between the parishes of Holne and Buckfastleigh.

Scorriton

Holy Brook

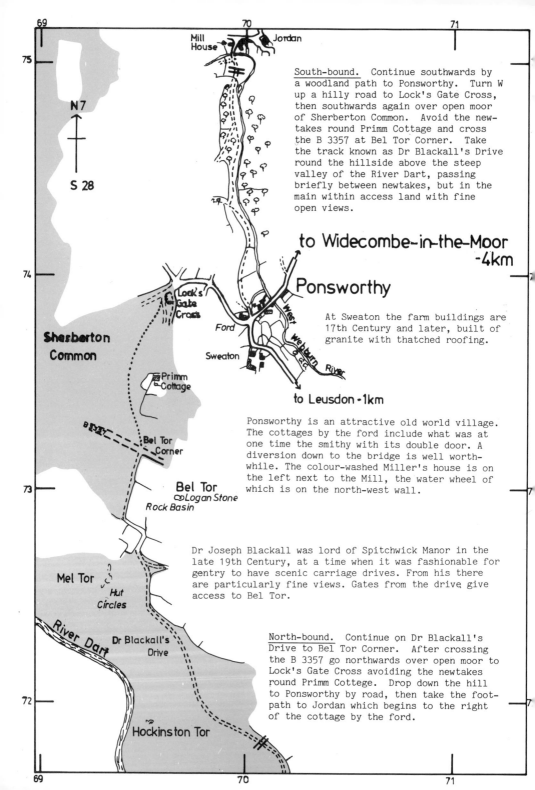

South-bound. Continue southwards by a woodland path to Ponsworthy. Turn W up a hilly road to Lock's Gate Cross, then southwards again over open moor of Sherberton Common. Avoid the new-takes round Primm Cottage and cross the B 3357 at Bel Tor Corner. Take the track known as Dr Blackall's Drive round the hillside above the steep valley of the River Dart, passing briefly between newtakes, but in the main within access land with fine open views.

to Widecombe-in-the-Moor -4km

Ponsworthy

At Sweaton the farm buildings are 17th Century and later, built of granite with thatched roofing.

to Leusdon - 1km

Ponsworthy is an attractive old world village. The cottages by the ford include what was at one time the smithy with its double door. A diversion down to the bridge is well worth-while. The colour-washed Miller's house is on the left next to the Mill, the water wheel of which is on the north-west wall.

Dr Joseph Blackall was lord of Spitchwick Manor in the late 19th Century, at a time when it was fashionable for gentry to have scenic carriage drives. From his there are particularly fine views. Gates from the drive give access to Bel Tor.

North-bound. Continue on Dr Blackall's Drive to Bel Tor Corner. After crossing the B 3357 go northwards over open moor to Lock's Gate Cross avoiding the newtakes round Primm Cottege. Drop down the hill to Ponsworthy by road, then take the foot-path to Jordan which begins to the right of the cottage by the ford.

Map labels: Mill House, Jordan, N 7, S 28, Sherberton Common, Lock's Gate Cross, Ford, Primm Cottage, Sweaton, West Webburn River, B 3357, Bel Tor Corner, Bel Tor, Logan Stone, Rock Basin, Mel Tor, Hut Circles, River Dart, Dr Blackall's Drive, Hockinston Tor

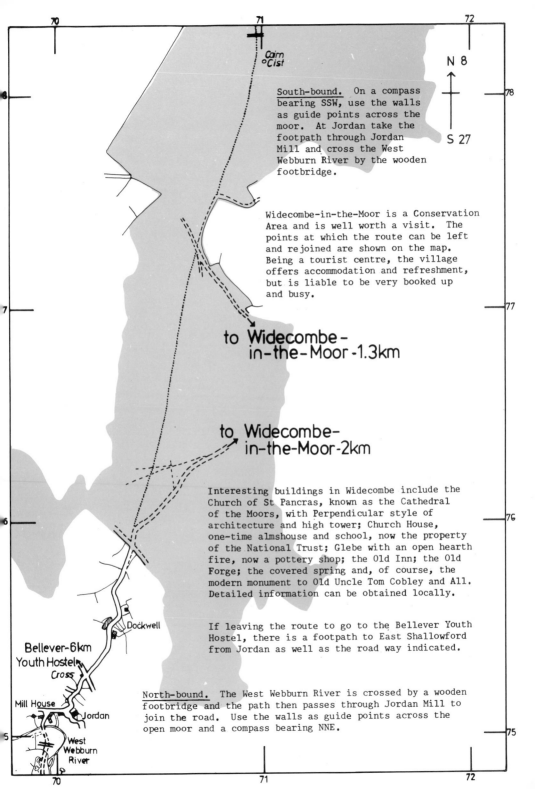

Cairn Cist

N 8

S 27

South-bound. On a compass bearing SSW, use the walls as guide points across the moor. At Jordan take the footpath through Jordan Mill and cross the West Webburn River by the wooden footbridge.

Widecombe-in-the-Moor is a Conservation Area and is well worth a visit. The points at which the route can be left and rejoined are shown on the map. Being a tourist centre, the village offers accommodation and refreshment, but is liable to be very booked up and busy.

to Widecombe-in-the-Moor -1.3km

to Widecombe-in-the-Moor-2km

Interesting buildings in Widecombe include the Church of St Pancras, known as the Cathedral of the Moors, with Perpendicular style of architecture and high tower; Church House, one-time almshouse and school, now the property of the National Trust; Glebe with an open hearth fire, now a pottery shop; the Old Inn; the Old Forge; the covered spring and, of course, the modern monument to Old Uncle Tom Cobley and All. Detailed information can be obtained locally.

If leaving the route to go to the Bellever Youth Hostel, there is a footpath to East Shallowford from Jordan as well as the road way indicated.

Dockwell

Bellever-6km
Youth Hostel
Cross

Mill House

Jordan

West Webburn River

North-bound. The West Webburn River is crossed by a wooden footbridge and the path then passes through Jordan Mill to join the road. Use the walls as guide points across the open moor and a compass bearing NNE.

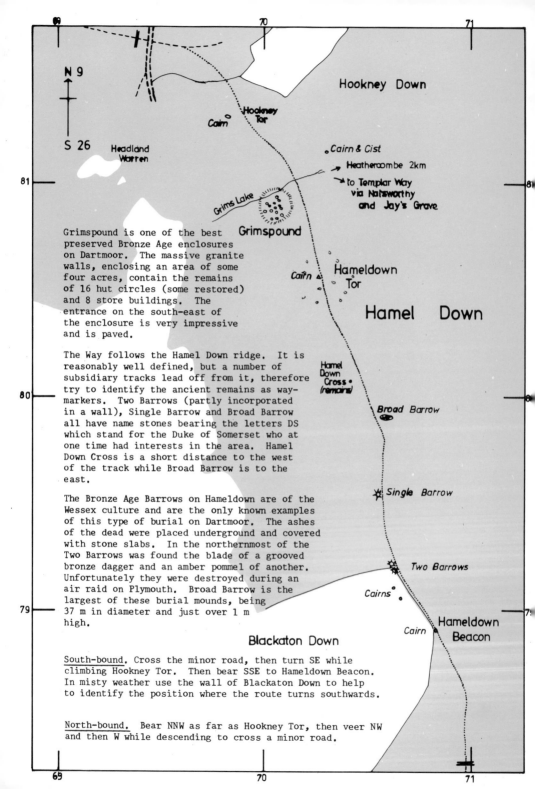

N 9

S 26

Hookney Down

Cairn

Hookney Tor

Headland Warren

Cairn & Cist

Heathercombe 2km

to Templar Way via Natsworthy and Jay's Grave

Grims Lake

Grimspound

Grimspound is one of the best
preserved Bronze Age enclosures
on Dartmoor. The massive granite
walls, enclosing an area of some
four acres, contain the remains
of 16 hut circles (some restored)
and 8 store buildings. The
entrance on the south-east of
the enclosure is very impressive
and is paved.

Cairn

Hameldown Tor

Hamel Down

The Way follows the Hamel Down ridge. It is
reasonably well defined, but a number of
subsidiary tracks lead off from it, therefore
try to identify the ancient remains as waymarkers. Two Barrows (partly incorporated
in a wall), Single Barrow and Broad Barrow
all have name stones bearing the letters DS
which stand for the Duke of Somerset who at
one time had interests in the area. Hamel
Down Cross is a short distance to the west
of the track while Broad Barrow is to the
east.

Hamel Down Cross (remains)

Broad Barrow

The Bronze Age Barrows on Hameldown are of the
Wessex culture and are the only known examples
of this type of burial on Dartmoor. The ashes
of the dead were placed underground and covered
with stone slabs. In the northernmost of the
Two Barrows was found the blade of a grooved
bronze dagger and an amber pommel of another.
Unfortunately they were destroyed during an
air raid on Plymouth. Broad Barrow is the
largest of these burial mounds, being
37 m in diameter and just over 1 m
high.

Single Barrow

Two Barrows

Cairns

Blackaton Down

Cairn

Hameldown Beacon

South-bound. Cross the minor road, then turn SE while
climbing Hookney Tor. Then bear SSE to Hameldown Beacon.
In misty weather use the wall of Blackaton Down to help
to identify the position where the route turns southwards.

North-bound. Bear NNW as far as Hookney Tor, then veer NW
and then W while descending to cross a minor road.

Double Stone Row
Chagford Common

Hut Circle
North Bovey Head

BRONZE AGE
ANTIQUITIES

Hamel Down Kistvaen

Grimspound

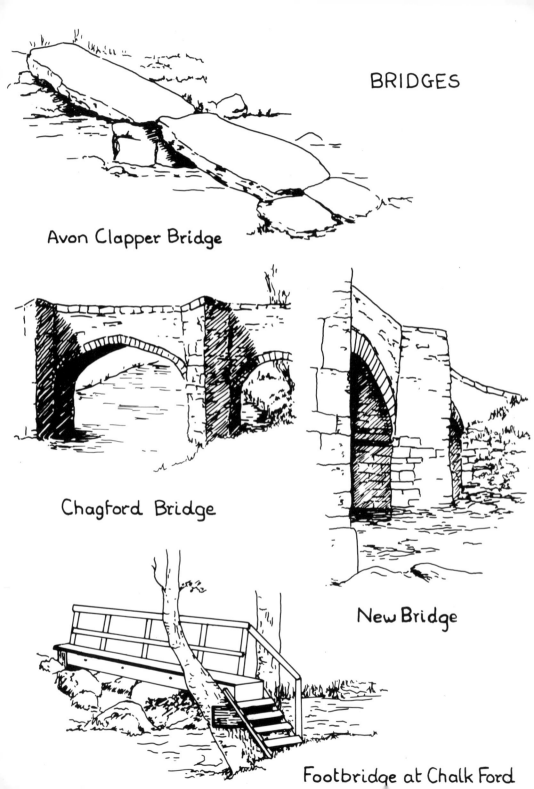

BRIDGES

Avon Clapper Bridge

Chagford Bridge

New Bridge

Footbridge at Chalk Ford

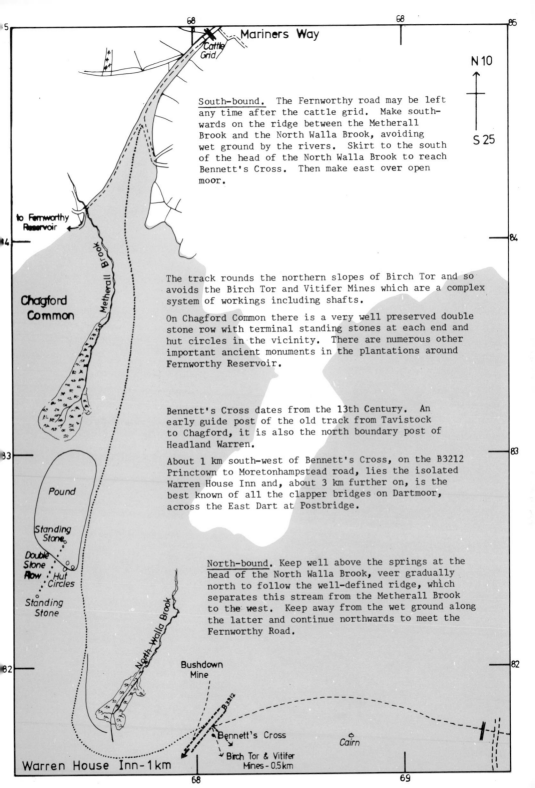

Mariners Way

Cattle Grid

N 10

S 25

South-bound. The Fernworthy road may be left any time after the cattle grid. Make south-wards on the ridge between the Metherall Brook and the North Walla Brook, avoiding wet ground by the rivers. Skirt to the south of the head of the North Walla Brook to reach Bennett's Cross. Then make east over open moor.

to Fernworthy Reservoir

Metherall Brook

Chagford Common

The track rounds the northern slopes of Birch Tor and so avoids the Birch Tor and Vitifer Mines which are a complex system of workings including shafts.

On Chagford Common there is a very well preserved double stone row with terminal standing stones at each end and hut circles in the vicinity. There are numerous other important ancient monuments in the plantations around Fernworthy Reservoir.

Bennett's Cross dates from the 13th Century. An early guide post of the old track from Tavistock to Chagford, it is also the north boundary post of Headland Warren.

About 1 km south-west of Bennett's Cross, on the B3212 Princtown to Moretonhampstead road, lies the isolated Warren House Inn and, about 3 km further on, is the best known of all the clapper bridges on Dartmoor, across the East Dart at Postbridge.

Pound

Standing Stone

Double Stone Row

Hut Circles

Standing Stone

North Walla Brook

North-bound. Keep well above the springs at the head of the North Walla Brook, veer gradually north to follow the well-defined ridge, which separates this stream from the Metherall Brook to the west. Keep away from the wet ground along the latter and continue northwards to meet the Fernworthy Road.

Bushdown Mine

B 3212

Cairn

Warren House Inn - 1 km

Bennett's Cross

Birch Tor & Vitifer Mines - 0.5km

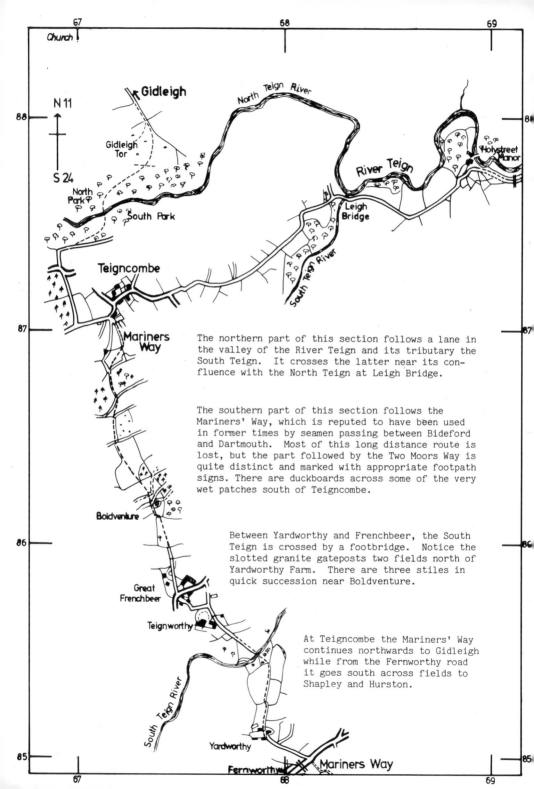

The northern part of this section follows a lane in the valley of the River Teign and its tributary the South Teign. It crosses the latter near its confluence with the North Teign at Leigh Bridge.

The southern part of this section follows the Mariners' Way, which is reputed to have been used in former times by seamen passing between Bideford and Dartmouth. Most of this long distance route is lost, but the part followed by the Two Moors Way is quite distinct and marked with appropriate footpath signs. There are duckboards across some of the very wet patches south of Teigncombe.

Between Yardworthy and Frenchbeer, the South Teign is crossed by a footbridge. Notice the slotted granite gateposts two fields north of Yardworthy Farm. There are three stiles in quick succession near Boldventure.

At Teigncombe the Mariners' Way continues northwards to Gidleigh while from the Fernworthy road it goes south across fields to Shapley and Hurston.

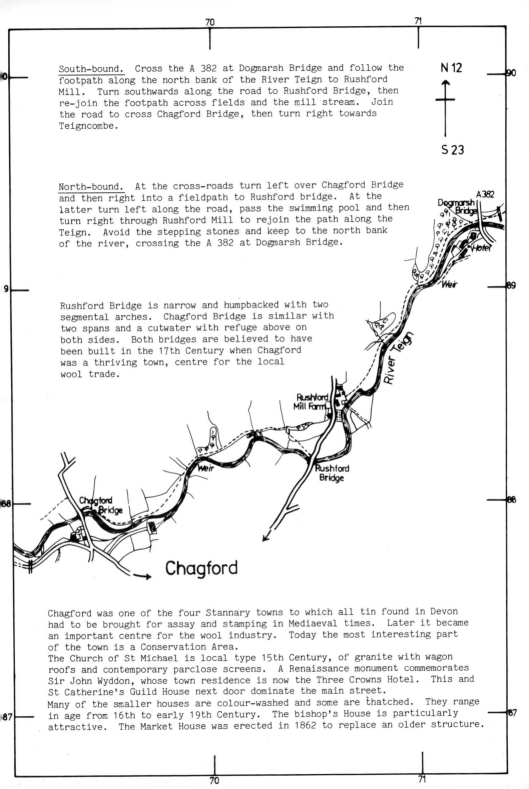

South-bound. Cross the A 382 at Dogmarsh Bridge and follow the
footpath along the north bank of the River Teign to Rushford
Mill. Turn southwards along the road to Rushford Bridge, then
re-join the footpath across fields and the mill stream. Join
the road to cross Chagford Bridge, then turn right towards
Teigncombe.

N 12

S 23

North-bound. At the cross-roads turn left over Chagford Bridge
and then right into a fieldpath to Rushford bridge. At the
latter turn left along the road, pass the swimming pool and then
turn right through Rushford Mill to rejoin the path along the
Teign. Avoid the stepping stones and keep to the north bank
of the river, crossing the A 382 at Dogmarsh Bridge.

A382

Dogmarsh
Bridge

Hotel

Weir

Rushford Bridge is narrow and humpbacked with two
segmental arches. Chagford Bridge is similar with
two spans and a cutwater with refuge above on
both sides. Both bridges are believed to have
been built in the 17th Century when Chagford
was a thriving town, centre for the local
wool trade.

River Teign

Rushford
Mill Farm

Weir

Rushford
Bridge

Chagford
Bridge

Chagford

Chagford was one of the four Stannary towns to which all tin found in Devon
had to be brought for assay and stamping in Mediaeval times. Later it became
an important centre for the wool industry. Today the most interesting part
of the town is a Conservation Area.
The Church of St Michael is local type 15th Century, of granite with wagon
roofs and contemporary parclose screens. A Renaissance monument commemorates
Sir John Wyddon, whose town residence is now the Three Crowns Hotel. This and
St Catherine's Guild House next door dominate the main street.
Many of the smaller houses are colour-washed and some are thatched. They range
in age from 16th to early 19th Century. The bishop's House is particularly
attractive. The Market House was erected in 1862 to replace an older structure.

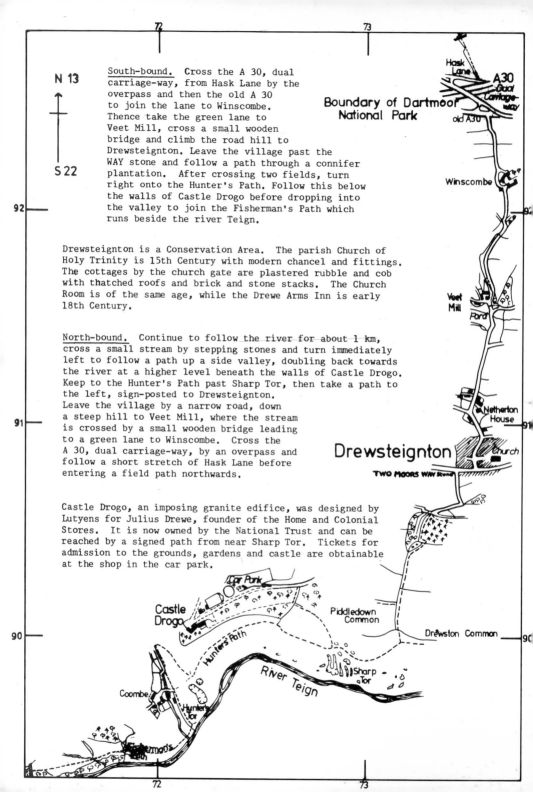

South-bound. Cross the A 30, dual carriage-way, from Hask Lane by the overpass and then the old A 30 to join the lane to Winscombe. Thence take the green lane to Veet Mill, cross a small wooden bridge and climb the road hill to Drewsteignton. Leave the village past the WAY stone and follow a path through a connifer plantation. After crossing two fields, turn right onto the Hunter's Path. Follow this below the walls of Castle Drogo before dropping into the valley to join the Fisherman's Path which runs beside the river Teign.

Drewsteignton is a Conservation Area. The parish Church of Holy Trinity is 15th Century with modern chancel and fittings. The cottages by the church gate are plastered rubble and cob with thatched roofs and brick and stone stacks. The Church Room is of the same age, while the Drewe Arms Inn is early 18th Century.

North-bound. Continue to follow the river for about 1 km, cross a small stream by stepping stones and turn immediately left to follow a path up a side valley, doubling back towards the river at a higher level beneath the walls of Castle Drogo. Keep to the Hunter's Path past Sharp Tor, then take a path to the left, sign-posted to Drewsteignton. Leave the village by a narrow road, down a steep hill to Veet Mill, where the stream is crossed by a small wooden bridge leading to a green lane to Winscombe. Cross the A 30, dual carriage-way, by an overpass and follow a short stretch of Hask Lane before entering a field path northwards.

Castle Drogo, an imposing granite edifice, was designed by Lutyens for Julius Drewe, founder of the Home and Colonial Stores. It is now owned by the National Trust and can be reached by a signed path from near Sharp Tor. Tickets for admission to the grounds, gardens and castle are obtainable at the shop in the car park.

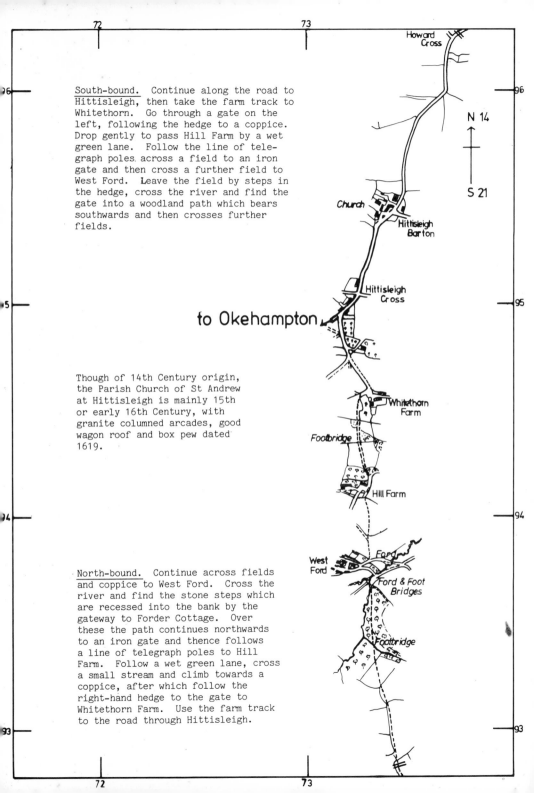

South-bound. Continue along the road to
Hittisleigh, then take the farm track to
Whitethorn. Go through a gate on the
left, following the hedge to a coppice.
Drop gently to pass Hill Farm by a wet
green lane. Follow the line of telegraph poles across a field to an iron
gate and then cross a further field to
West Ford. Leave the field by steps in
the hedge, cross the river and find the
gate into a woodland path which bears
southwards and then crosses further
fields.

Though of 14th Century origin,
the Parish Church of St Andrew
at Hittisleigh is mainly 15th
or early 16th Century, with
granite columned arcades, good
wagon roof and box pew dated
1619.

North-bound. Continue across fields
and coppice to West Ford. Cross the
river and find the stone steps which
are recessed into the bank by the
gateway to Forder Cottage. Over
these the path continues northwards
to an iron gate and thence follows
a line of telegraph poles to Hill
Farm. Follow a wet green lane, cross
a small stream and climb towards a
coppice, after which follow the
right-hand hedge to the gate to
Whitethorn Farm. Use the farm track
to the road through Hittisleigh.

to Okehampton

Howard Cross

N 14

S 21

Church

Hittisleigh Barton

Hittisleigh Cross

Whitethorn Farm

Footbridge

Hill Farm

West Ford

Ford

Ford & Foot Bridges

Footbridge

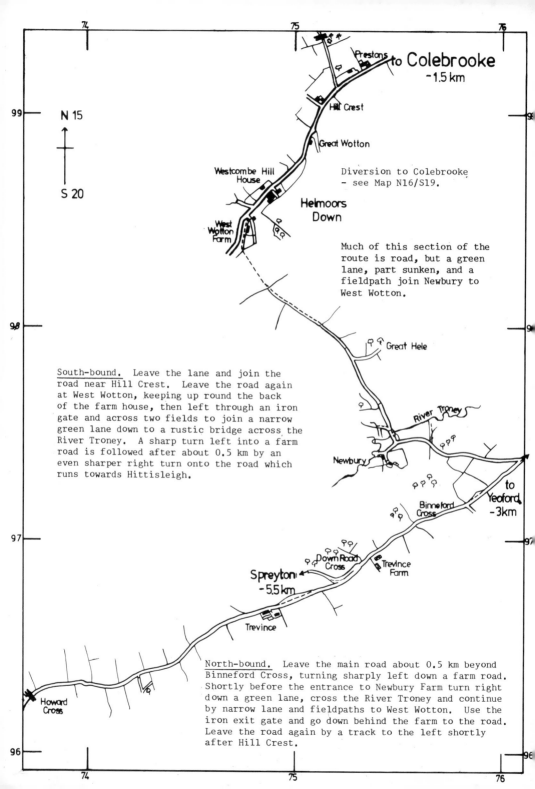

to **Colebrooke**
—1.5 km

Prestons

Hill Crest

N 15
↑
S 20

Great Wotton

Westcombe Hill
House

Diversion to Colebrooke
— see Map N16/S19.

Helmoors
Down

West
Wotton
Farm

Much of this section of the
route is road, but a green
lane, part sunken, and a
fieldpath join Newbury to
West Wotton.

Great Hele

South-bound. Leave the lane and join the
road near Hill Crest. Leave the road again
at West Wotton, keeping up round the back
of the farm house, then left through an iron
gate and across two fields to join a narrow
green lane down to a rustic bridge across the
River Troney. A sharp turn left into a farm
road is followed after about 0.5 km by an
even sharper right turn onto the road which
runs towards Hittisleigh.

River Troney

Newbury

to
Yeoford
—3km

Binneford
Cross

Down Road
Cross

Trevince
Farm

Spreyton
—5.5km

Trevince

Howard
Cross

North-bound. Leave the main road about 0.5 km beyond
Binneford Cross, turning sharply left down a farm road.
Shortly before the entrance to Newbury Farm turn right
down a green lane, cross the River Troney and continue
by narrow lane and fieldpaths to West Wotton. Use the
iron exit gate and go down behind the farm to the road.
Leave the road again by a track to the left shortly
after Hill Crest.

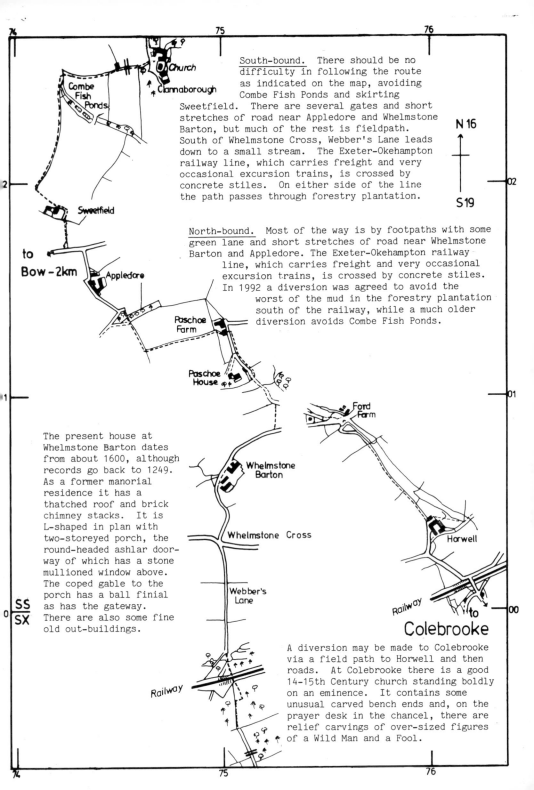

South-bound. There should be no difficulty in following the route as indicated on the map, avoiding Combe Fish Ponds and skirting Sweetfield. There are several gates and short stretches of road near Appledore and Whelmstone Barton, but much of the rest is fieldpath. South of Whelmstone Cross, Webber's Lane leads down to a small stream. The Exeter-Okehampton railway line, which carries freight and very occasional excursion trains, is crossed by concrete stiles. On either side of the line the path passes through forestry plantation.

North-bound. Most of the way is by footpaths with some green lane and short stretches of road near Whelmstone Barton and Appledore. The Exeter-Okehampton railway line, which carries freight and very occasional excursion trains, is crossed by concrete stiles. In 1992 a diversion was agreed to avoid the worst of the mud in the forestry plantation south of the railway, while a much older diversion avoids Combe Fish Ponds.

The present house at Whelmstone Barton dates from about 1600, although records go back to 1249. As a former manorial residence it has a thatched roof and brick chimney stacks. It is L-shaped in plan with two-storeyed porch, the round-headed ashlar doorway of which has a stone mullioned window above. The coped gable to the porch has a ball finial as has the gateway. There are also some fine old out-buildings.

A diversion may be made to Colebrooke via a field path to Horwell and then roads. At Colebrooke there is a good 14-15th Century church standing boldly on an eminence. It contains some unusual carved bench ends and, on the prayer desk in the chancel, there are relief carvings of over-sized figures of a Wild Man and a Fool.

N 16

S 19

Church
Clannaborough
Combe Fish Ponds
Sweetfield
to Bow - 2km
Appledore
Paschoe Farm
Paschoe House
Ford Farm
Whelmstone Barton
Whelmstone Cross
Horwell
Webber's Lane
Railway
Railway
to Colebrooke
Colebrooke

SS SX

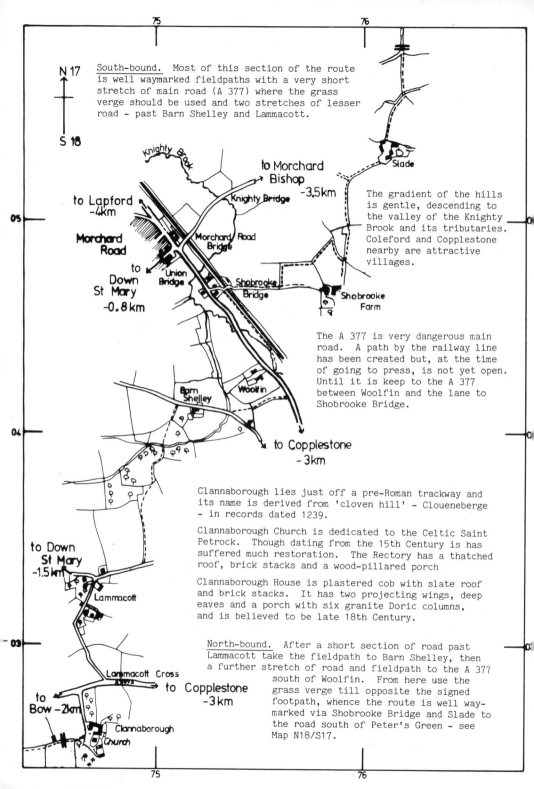

South-bound. Most of this section of the route is well waymarked fieldpaths with a very short stretch of main road (A 377) where the grass verge should be used and two stretches of lesser road - past Barn Shelley and Lammacott.

Knighty Brook

to Morchard Bishop
-3.5km

Knighty Bridge

to Lapford -4km

Morchard Road

Morchard Road Bridge

to Down St Mary -0.8km

Union Bridge

Shobrooke Bridge

Slade

The gradient of the hills is gentle, descending to the valley of the Knighty Brook and its tributaries. Coleford and Copplestone nearby are attractive villages.

Shobrooke Farm

Barn Shelley

Woolfin

The A 377 is very dangerous main road. A path by the railway line has been created but, at the time of going to press, is not yet open. Until it is keep to the A 377 between Woolfin and the lane to Shobrooke Bridge.

to Copplestone -3km

Clannaborough lies just off a pre-Roman trackway and its name is derived from 'cloven hill' - Cloueneberge - in records dated 1239.

Clannaborough Church is dedicated to the Celtic Saint Petrock. Though dating from the 15th Century is has suffered much restoration. The Rectory has a thatched roof, brick stacks and a wood-pillared porch

Clannaborough House is plastered cob with slate roof and brick stacks. It has two projecting wings, deep eaves and a porch with six granite Doric columns, and is believed to be late 18th Century.

to Down St Mary -1.5 km

Lammacott

Lammacott Cross

to Copplestone -3km

to Bow -2km

Clannaborough Church

North-bound. After a short section of road past Lammacott take the fieldpath to Barn Shelley, then a further stretch of road and fieldpath to the A 377 south of Woolfin. From here use the grass verge till opposite the signed footpath, whence the route is well way-marked via Shobrooke Bridge and Slade to the road south of Peter's Green - see Map N18/S17.

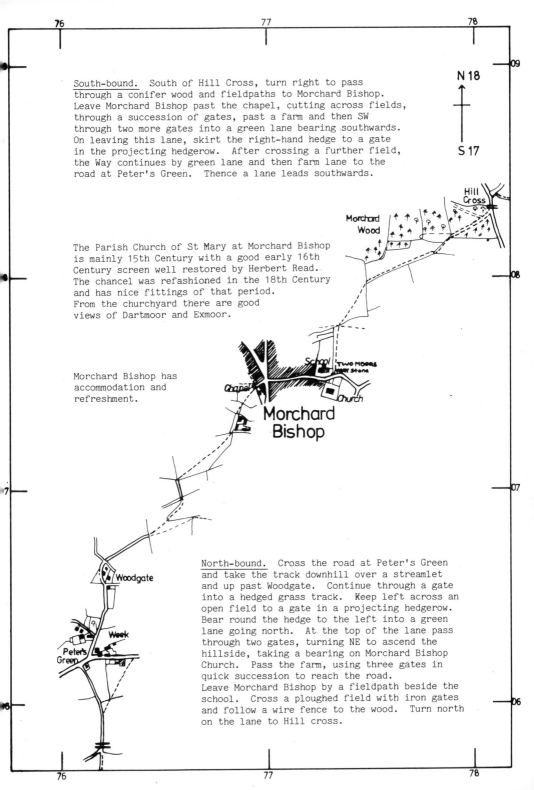

South-bound. South of Hill Cross, turn right to pass through a conifer wood and fieldpaths to Morchard Bishop. Leave Morchard Bishop past the chapel, cutting across fields, through a succession of gates, past a farm and then SW through two more gates into a green lane bearing southwards. On leaving this lane, skirt the right-hand hedge to a gate in the projecting hedgerow. After crossing a further field, the Way continues by green lane and then farm lane to the road at Peter's Green. Thence a lane leads southwards.

The Parish Church of St Mary at Morchard Bishop is mainly 15th Century with a good early 16th Century screen well restored by Herbert Read. The chancel was refashioned in the 18th Century and has nice fittings of that period. From the churchyard there are good views of Dartmoor and Exmoor.

Morchard Bishop has accommodation and refreshment.

North-bound. Cross the road at Peter's Green and take the track downhill over a streamlet and up past Woodgate. Continue through a gate into a hedged grass track. Keep left across an open field to a gate in a projecting hedgerow. Bear round the hedge to the left into a green lane going north. At the top of the lane pass through two gates, turning NE to ascend the hillside, taking a bearing on Morchard Bishop Church. Pass the farm, using three gates in quick succession to reach the road. Leave Morchard Bishop by a fieldpath beside the school. Cross a ploughed field with iron gates and follow a wire fence to the wood. Turn north on the lane to Hill cross.

N 18

S 17

Hill Cross

Morchard Wood

School

TWO MOORS WAY Stone

Chapel

Church

Morchard Bishop

Woodgate

Week

Peter's Green

76   77   78

09   08   07   06

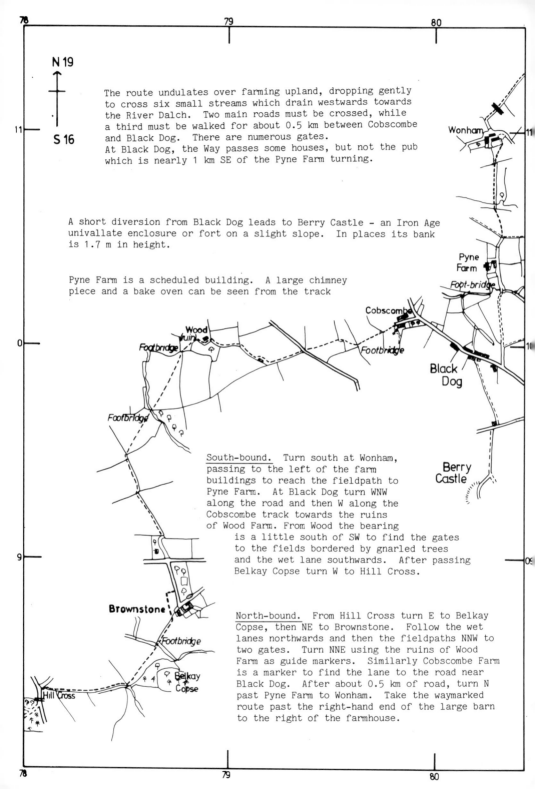

The route undulates over farming upland, dropping gently
to cross six small streams which drain westwards towards
the River Dalch. Two main roads must be crossed, while
a third must be walked for about 0.5 km between Cobscombe
and Black Dog. There are numerous gates.
At Black Dog, the Way passes some houses, but not the pub
which is nearly 1 km SE of the Pyne Farm turning.

A short diversion from Black Dog leads to Berry Castle - an Iron Age
univallate enclosure or fort on a slight slope. In places its bank
is 1.7 m in height.

Pyne Farm is a scheduled building. A large chimney
piece and a bake oven can be seen from the track

Wonham

Pyne
Farm

Foot-bridge

Cobscombe

Wood
ruins

Footbridge

Footbridge

Footbridge

Black
Dog

Berry
Castle

South-bound. Turn south at Wonham,
passing to the left of the farm
buildings to reach the fieldpath to
Pyne Farm. At Black Dog turn WNW
along the road and then W along the
Cobscombe track towards the ruins
of Wood Farm. From Wood the bearing
is a little south of SW to find the gates
to the fields bordered by gnarled trees
and the wet lane southwards. After passing
Belkay Copse turn W to Hill Cross.

Brownstone

Footbridge

Belkay
Copse

Hill Cross

North-bound. From Hill Cross turn E to Belkay
Copse, then NE to Brownstone. Follow the wet
lanes northwards and then the fieldpaths NNW to
two gates. Turn NNE using the ruins of Wood
Farm as guide markers. Similarly Cobscombe Farm
is a marker to find the lane to the road near
Black Dog. After about 0.5 km of road, turn N
past Pyne Farm to Wonham. Take the waymarked
route past the right-hand end of the large barn
to the right of the farmhouse.

CHURCHES

Drewsteignton

Washford Pyne

Font at
Hittisleigh

Morchard Bishop

WAYSIDE
INNS

Church House Inn
Holne

Drewe Arms
Drewsteignton

Abandoned
Cider Press

Mason's Arms
Knowstone

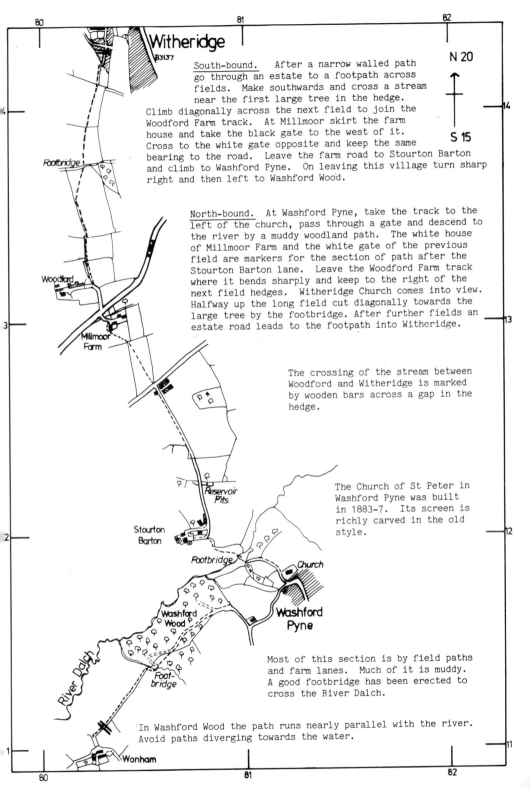

Witheridge

B3137

South-bound. After a narrow walled path go through an estate to a footpath across fields. Make southwards and cross a stream near the first large tree in the hedge. Climb diagonally across the next field to join the Woodford Farm track. At Millmoor skirt the farm house and take the black gate to the west of it. Cross to the white gate opposite and keep the same bearing to the road. Leave the farm road to Stourton Barton and climb to Washford Pyne. On leaving this village turn sharp right and then left to Washford Wood.

North-bound. At Washford Pyne, take the track to the left of the church, pass through a gate and descend to the river by a muddy woodland path. The white house of Millmoor Farm and the white gate of the previous field are markers for the section of path after the Stourton Barton lane. Leave the Woodford Farm track where it bends sharply and keep to the right of the next field hedges. Witheridge Church comes into view. Halfway up the long field cut diagonally towards the large tree by the footbridge. After further fields an estate road leads to the footpath into Witheridge.

The crossing of the stream between Woodford and Witheridge is marked by wooden bars across a gap in the hedge.

The Church of St Peter in Washford Pyne was built in 1883-7. Its screen is richly carved in the old style.

Most of this section is by field paths and farm lanes. Much of it is muddy. A good footbridge has been erected to cross the River Dalch.

In Washford Wood the path runs nearly parallel with the river. Avoid paths diverging towards the water.

N 20

S 15

Footbridge

Woodford

Millmoor Farm

Reservoir Pits

Stourton Barton

Footbridge

Washford Wood

Washford Pyne

Church

Foot-bridge

River Dalch

Wonham

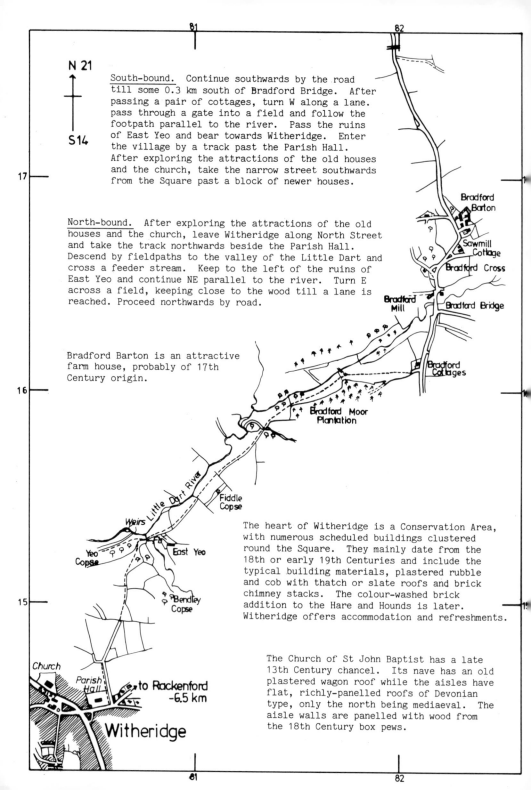

N 21

S 14

South-bound. Continue southwards by the road till some 0.3 km south of Bradford Bridge. After passing a pair of cottages, turn W along a lane. pass through a gate into a field and follow the footpath parallel to the river. Pass the ruins of East Yeo and bear towards Witheridge. Enter the village by a track past the Parish Hall. After exploring the attractions of the old houses and the church, take the narrow street southwards from the Square past a block of newer houses.

North-bound. After exploring the attractions of the old houses and the church, leave Witheridge along North Street and take the track northwards beside the Parish Hall. Descend by fieldpaths to the valley of the Little Dart and cross a feeder stream. Keep to the left of the ruins of East Yeo and continue NE parallel to the river. Turn E across a field, keeping close to the wood till a lane is reached. Proceed northwards by road.

Bradford Barton is an attractive farm house, probably of 17th Century origin.

The heart of Witheridge is a Conservation Area, with numerous scheduled buildings clustered round the Square. They mainly date from the 18th or early 19th Centuries and include the typical building materials, plastered rubble and cob with thatch or slate roofs and brick chimney stacks. The colour-washed brick addition to the Hare and Hounds is later. Witheridge offers accommodation and refreshments.

The Church of St John Baptist has a late 13th Century chancel. Its nave has an old plastered wagon roof while the aisles have flat, richly-panelled roofs of Devonian type, only the north being mediaeval. The aisle walls are panelled with wood from the 18th Century box pews.

Bradford Barton

Sawmill Cottage

Bradford Cross

Bradford Mill

Bradford Bridge

Bradford Cottages

Bradford Moor Plantation

Little Dart River

Weirs

Fiddle Copse

Yeo Copse

East Yeo

Bendley Copse

Church

Parish Hall

to Rackenford -6.5 km

Witheridge

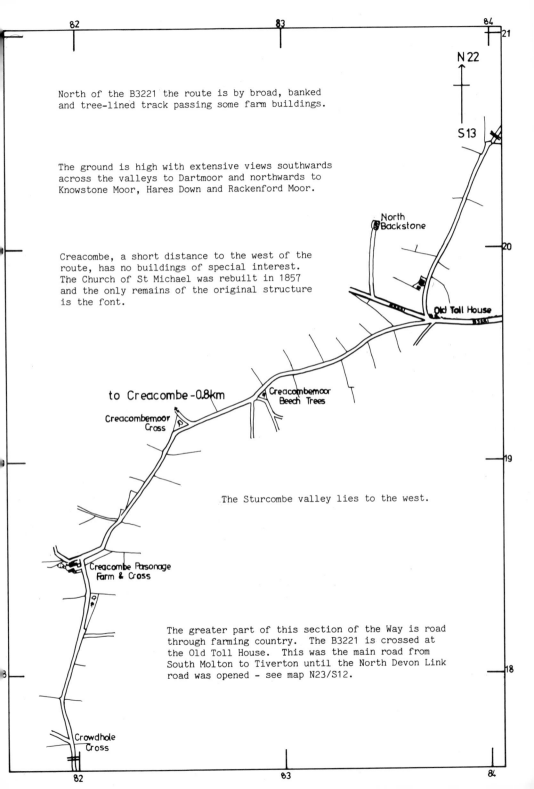

North of the B3221 the route is by broad, banked and tree-lined track passing some farm buildings.

The ground is high with extensive views southwards across the valleys to Dartmoor and northwards to Knowstone Moor, Hares Down and Rackenford Moor.

Creacombe, a short distance to the west of the route, has no buildings of special interest. The Church of St Michael was rebuilt in 1857 and the only remains of the original structure is the font.

The Sturcombe valley lies to the west.

The greater part of this section of the Way is road through farming country. The B3221 is crossed at the Old Toll House. This was the main road from South Molton to Tiverton until the North Devon Link road was opened - see map N23/S12.

N 22

S 13

North Backstone

Old Toll House

to Creacombe - 0.8km

Creacombemoor Beech Trees

Creacombemoor Cross

Creacombe Parsonage Farm & Cross

Crowdhole Cross

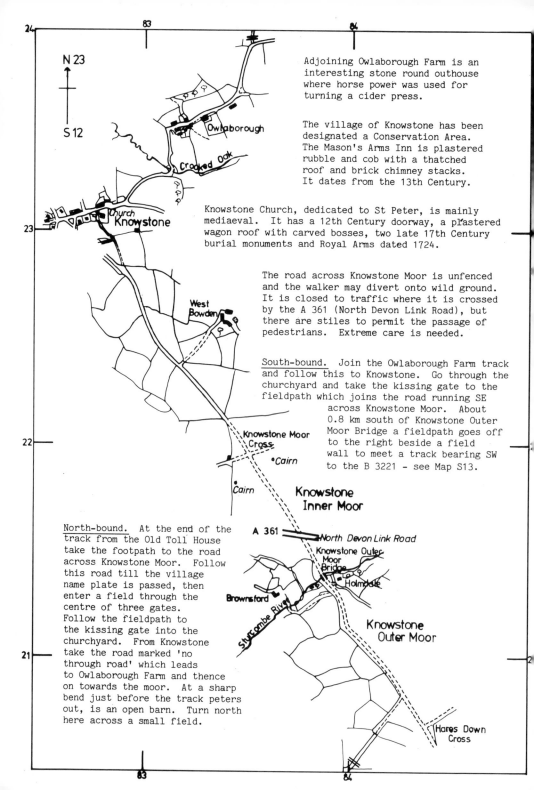

Adjoining Owlaborough Farm is an interesting stone round outhouse where horse power was used for turning a cider press.

The village of Knowstone has been designated a Conservation Area. The Mason's Arms Inn is plastered rubble and cob with a thatched roof and brick chimney stacks. It dates from the 13th Century.

Knowstone Church, dedicated to St Peter, is mainly mediaeval. It has a 12th Century doorway, a plastered wagon roof with carved bosses, two late 17th Century burial monuments and Royal Arms dated 1724.

The road across Knowstone Moor is unfenced and the walker may divert onto wild ground. It is closed to traffic where it is crossed by the A 361 (North Devon Link Road), but there are stiles to permit the passage of pedestrians. Extreme care is needed.

South-bound. Join the Owlaborough Farm track and follow this to Knowstone. Go through the churchyard and take the kissing gate to the fieldpath which joins the road running SE across Knowstone Moor. About 0.8 km south of Knowstone Outer Moor Bridge a fieldpath goes off to the right beside a field wall to meet a track bearing SW to the B 3221 - see Map S13.

North-bound. At the end of the track from the Old Toll House take the footpath to the road across Knowstone Moor. Follow this road till the village name plate is passed, then enter a field through the centre of three gates. Follow the fieldpath to the kissing gate into the churchyard. From Knowstone take the road marked 'no through road' which leads to Owlaborough Farm and thence on towards the moor. At a sharp bend just before the track peters out, is an open barn. Turn north here across a small field.

Owlaborough

Crooked Oak

Church
Knowstone

West
Bowden

Knowstone Moor
Cross

Cairn

Cairn

Knowstone
Inner Moor

A 361 — North Devon Link Road

Knowstone Outer
Moor
Bridge

Holmdale

Brownsford

Sturcombe River

Knowstone
Outer Moor

Hares Down
Cross

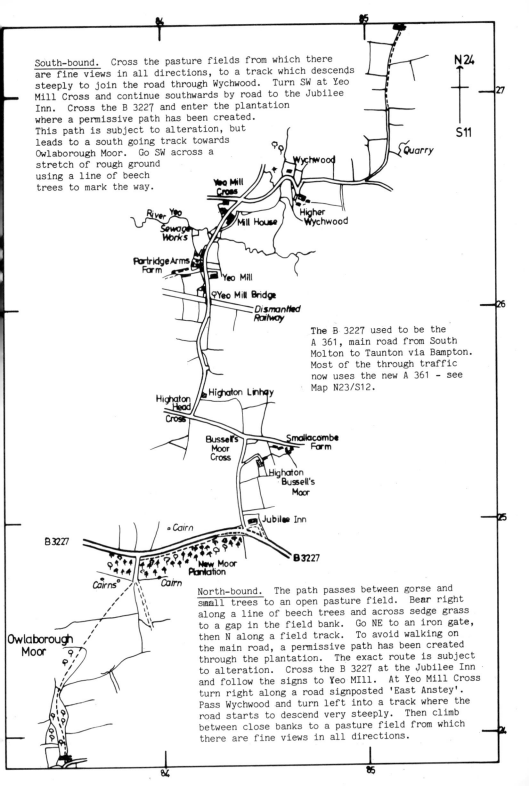

South-bound. Cross the pasture fields from which there are fine views in all directions, to a track which descends steeply to join the road through Wychwood. Turn SW at Yeo Mill Cross and continue southwards by road to the Jubilee Inn. Cross the B 3227 and enter the plantation where a permissive path has been created. This path is subject to alteration, but leads to a south going track towards Owlaborough Moor. Go SW across a stretch of rough ground using a line of beech trees to mark the way.

N 24

S 11

Quarry

Wychwood

Yeo Mill Cross

River Yeo

Sewage Works

Mill House

Higher Wychwood

Partridge Arms Farm

Yeo Mill

Yeo Mill Bridge

Dismantled Railway

The B 3227 used to be the A 361, main road from South Molton to Taunton via Bampton. Most of the through traffic now uses the new A 361 - see Map N23/S12.

Highaton Linhay

Highaton Head Cross

Bussel's Moor Cross

Smallacombe Farm

Highaton Bussell's Moor

Jubilee Inn

Cairn

B 3227

B 3227

Cairns

Cairn

New Moor Plantation

Owlaborough Moor

North-bound. The path passes between gorse and small trees to an open pasture field. Bear right along a line of beech trees and across sedge grass to a gap in the field bank. Go NE to an iron gate, then N along a field track. To avoid walking on the main road, a permissive path has been created through the plantation. The exact route is subject to alteration. Cross the B 3227 at the Jubilee Inn and follow the signs to Yeo MIll. At Yeo Mill Cross turn right along a road signposted 'East Anstey'. Pass Wychwood and turn left into a track where the road starts to descend very steeply. Then climb between close banks to a pasture field from which there are fine views in all directions.

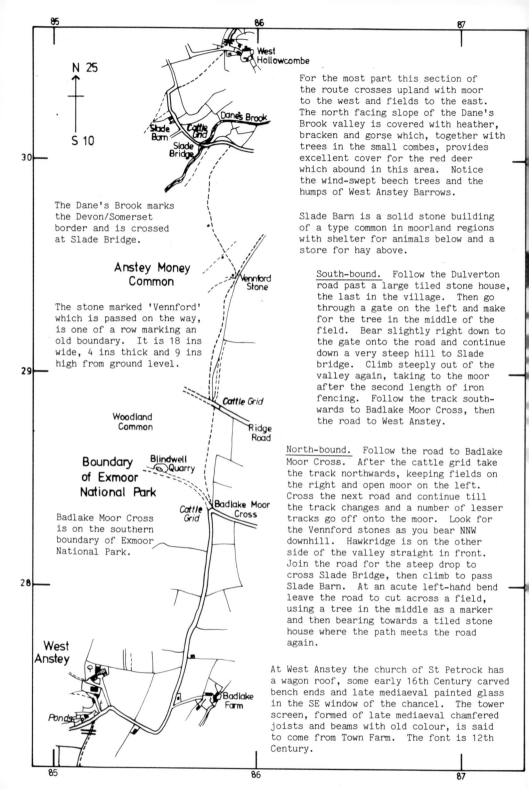

N 25

S 10

The Dane's Brook marks
the Devon/Somerset
border and is crossed
at Slade Bridge.

Anstey Money Common

The stone marked 'Vennford'
which is passed on the way,
is one of a row marking an
old boundary. It is 18 ins
wide, 4 ins thick and 9 ins
high from ground level.

Woodland
Common

Boundary of Exmoor National Park

Badlake Moor Cross
is on the southern
boundary of Exmoor
National Park.

West
Anstey

Ponds

West
Hollowcombe

Dane's Brook

Slade
Barn

Cattle
Grid

Slade
Bridge

Vennford
Stone

Cattle Grid

Ridge
Road

Blindwell
Quarry

Cattle
Grid

Badlake Moor
Cross

Badlake
Farm

For the most part this section of
the route crosses upland with moor
to the west and fields to the east.
The north facing slope of the Dane's
Brook valley is covered with heather,
bracken and gorse which, together with
trees in the small combes, provides
excellent cover for the red deer
which abound in this area. Notice
the wind-swept beech trees and the
humps of West Anstey Barrows.

Slade Barn is a solid stone building
of a type common in moorland regions
with shelter for animals below and a
store for hay above.

South-bound. Follow the Dulverton
road past a large tiled stone house,
the last in the village. Then go
through a gate on the left and make
for the tree in the middle of the
field. Bear slightly right down to
the gate onto the road and continue
down a very steep hill to Slade
bridge. Climb steeply out of the
valley again, taking to the moor
after the second length of iron
fencing. Follow the track southwards to Badlake Moor Cross, then
the road to West Anstey.

North-bound. Follow the road to Badlake
Moor Cross. After the cattle grid take
the track northwards, keeping fields on
the right and open moor on the left.
Cross the next road and continue till
the track changes and a number of lesser
tracks go off onto the moor. Look for
the Vennford stones as you bear NNW
downhill. Hawkridge is on the other
side of the valley straight in front.
Join the road for the steep drop to
cross Slade Bridge, then climb to pass
Slade Barn. At an acute left-hand bend
leave the road to cut across a field,
using a tree in the middle as a marker
and then bearing towards a tiled stone
house where the path meets the road
again.

At West Anstey the church of St Petrock has
a wagon roof, some early 16th Century carved
bench ends and late mediaeval painted glass
in the SE window of the chancel. The tower
screen, formed of late mediaeval chamfered
joists and beams with old colour, is said
to come from Town Farm. The font is 12th
Century.

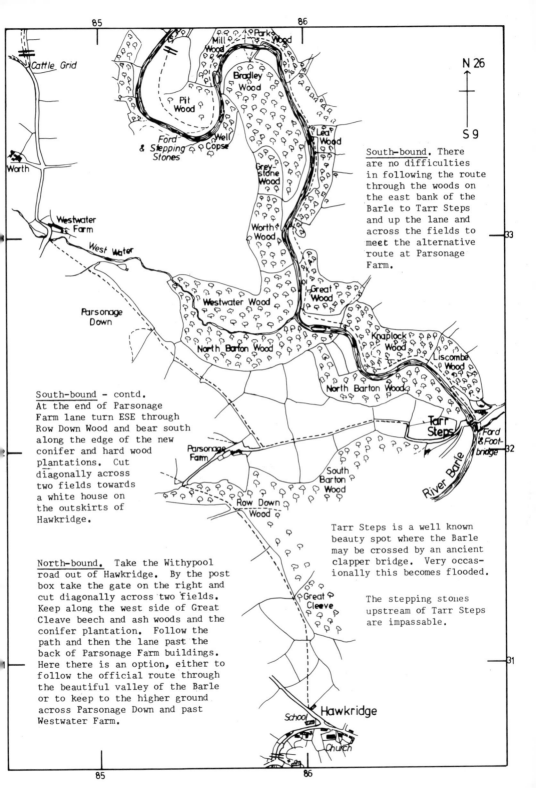

N 26

S 9

South-bound. There are no difficulties in following the route through the woods on the east bank of the Barle to Tarr Steps and up the lane and across the fields to meet the alternative route at Parsonage Farm.

South-bound — contd.
At the end of Parsonage Farm lane turn ESE through Row Down Wood and bear south along the edge of the new conifer and hard wood plantations. Cut diagonally across two fields towards a white house on the outskirts of Hawkridge.

North-bound. Take the Withypool road out of Hawkridge. By the post box take the gate on the right and cut diagonally across two fields. Keep along the west side of Great Cleave beech and ash woods and the conifer plantation. Follow the path and then the lane past the back of Parsonage Farm buildings. Here there is an option, either to follow the official route through the beautiful valley of the Barle or to keep to the higher ground across Parsonage Down and past Westwater Farm.

Tarr Steps is a well known beauty spot where the Barle may be crossed by an ancient clapper bridge. Very occasionally this becomes flooded.

The stepping stones upstream of Tarr Steps are impassable.

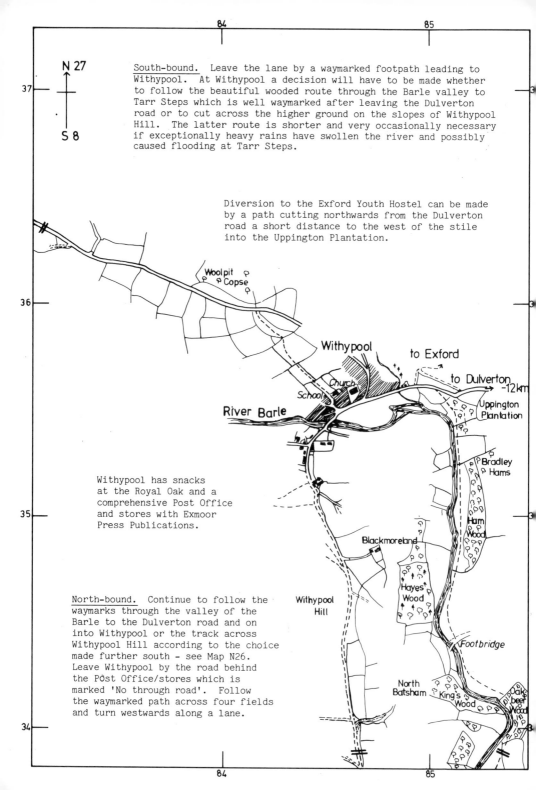

N 27

S 8

South-bound. Leave the lane by a waymarked footpath leading to Withypool. At Withypool a decision will have to be made whether to follow the beautiful wooded route through the Barle valley to Tarr Steps which is well waymarked after leaving the Dulverton road or to cut across the higher ground on the slopes of Withypool Hill. The latter route is shorter and very occasionally necessary if exceptionally heavy rains have swollen the river and possibly caused flooding at Tarr Steps.

Diversion to the Exford Youth Hostel can be made by a path cutting northwards from the Dulverton road a short distance to the west of the stile into the Uppington Plantation.

Woolpit Copse

Withypool

to Exford

to Dulverton
-12km

Church

School

Uppington Plantation

River Barle

Bradley Hams

Withypool has snacks at the Royal Oak and a comprehensive Post Office and stores with Exmoor Press Publications.

Ham Wood

Blackmoreland

Hayes Wood

North-bound. Continue to follow the waymarks through the valley of the Barle to the Dulverton road and on into Withypool or the track across Withypool Hill according to the choice made further south - see Map N26. Leave Withypool by the road behind the Post Office/stores which is marked 'No through road'. Follow the waymarked path across four fields and turn westwards along a lane.

Withypool Hill

Footbridge

North Batsham

King's Wood

Oaksbeer Wood

RURAL BUILDINGS

The Old Smithy ~
Ponsworthy

Farmhouse with Porch ~
Dockwell

Granite Trough & Ruin
of Great Frenchbeer

Thatched House in Drewsteignton

Bolt from the
Redlake Tramway

Various Other Points
of Interest you may
notice on the Way

Porch of the Longhouse
at Yardworthy

Field Stile & Wall Stile
on the Mariners' Way

Ash House & Gatepost
at Bradford Tracey

Castle Drogo above
the Teign Gorge

Hoar Oak marking the
Devon/Somerset Border

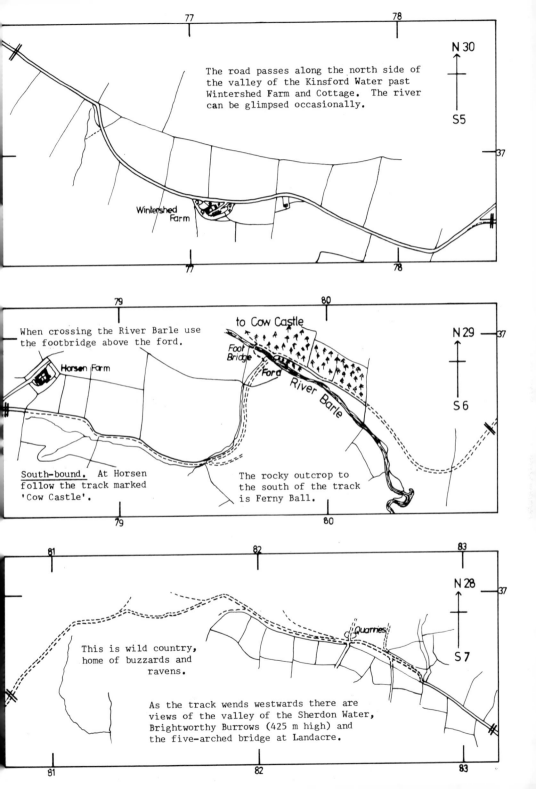

Panel 1

77   78   N 30 ↑ S5   37

The road passes along the north side of
the valley of the Kinsford Water past
Wintershed Farm and Cottage. The river
can be glimpsed occasionally.

Wintershed Farm

77   78

Panel 2

79   80   to Cow Castle   N 29 ↑ S 6   37

When crossing the River Barle use
the footbridge above the ford.

Horsen Farm

Foot Bridge

Ford   River Barle

South-bound. At Horsen
follow the track marked
'Cow Castle'.

The rocky outcrop to
the south of the track
is Ferny Ball.

79   80

Panel 3

81   82   83   N 28 ↑ S 7   37

Quarries

This is wild country,
home of buzzards and
ravens.

As the track wends westwards there are
views of the valley of the Sherdon Water,
Brightworthy Burrows (425 m high) and
the five-arched bridge at Landacre.

81   82   83

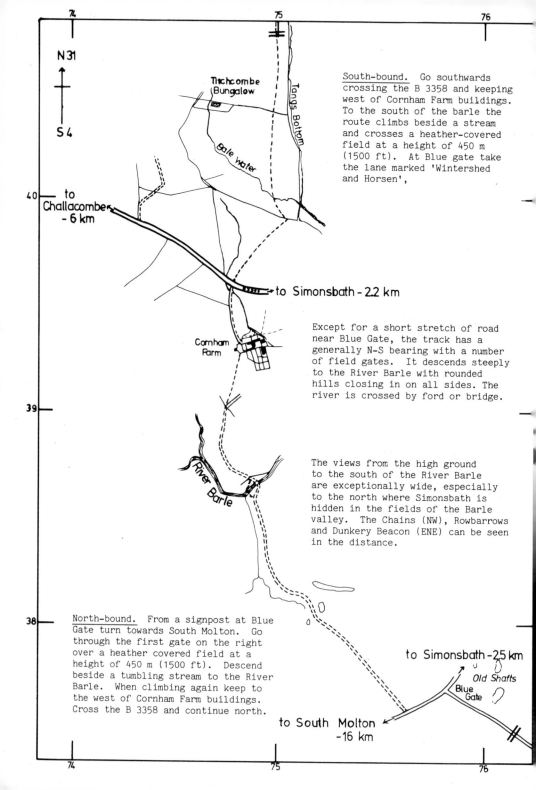

N 31

S 4

Titchcombe Bungalow

Tangs Bottom

Barle water

to Challacombe - 6 km

to Simonsbath - 2.2 km

Cornham Farm

River Barle

South-bound. Go southwards crossing the B 3358 and keeping west of Cornham Farm buildings. To the south of the barle the route climbs beside a stream and crosses a heather-covered field at a height of 450 m (1500 ft). At Blue gate take the lane marked 'Wintershed and Horsen',

Except for a short stretch of road near Blue Gate, the track has a generally N-S bearing with a number of field gates. It descends steeply to the River Barle with rounded hills closing in on all sides. The river is crossed by ford or bridge.

The views from the high ground to the south of the River Barle are exceptionally wide, especially to the north where Simonsbath is hidden in the fields of the Barle valley. The Chains (NW), Rowbarrows and Dunkery Beacon (ENE) can be seen in the distance.

North-bound. From a signpost at Blue Gate turn towards South Molton. Go through the first gate on the right over a heather covered field at a height of 450 m (1500 ft). Descend beside a tumbling stream to the River Barle. When climbing again keep to the west of Cornham Farm buildings. Cross the B 3358 and continue north.

to Simonsbath - 2.5 km

Old Shafts

Blue Gate

to South Molton - 16 km

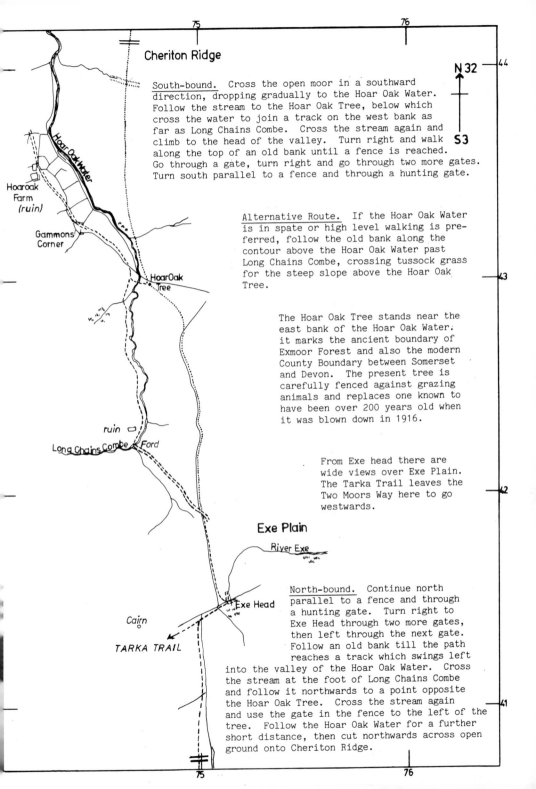

Cheriton Ridge

N 32

S3

South-bound. Cross the open moor in a southward direction, dropping gradually to the Hoar Oak Water. Follow the stream to the Hoar Oak Tree, below which cross the water to join a track on the west bank as far as Long Chains Combe. Cross the stream again and climb to the head of the valley. Turn right and walk along the top of an old bank until a fence is reached. Go through a gate, turn right and go through two more gates. Turn south parallel to a fence and through a hunting gate.

Alternative Route. If the Hoar Oak Water is in spate or high level walking is preferred, follow the old bank along the contour above the Hoar Oak Water past Long Chains Combe, crossing tussock grass for the steep slope above the Hoar Oak Tree.

The Hoar Oak Tree stands near the east bank of the Hoar Oak Water: it marks the ancient boundary of Exmoor Forest and also the modern County Boundary between Somerset and Devon. The present tree is carefully fenced against grazing animals and replaces one known to have been over 200 years old when it was blown down in 1916.

From Exe head there are wide views over Exe Plain. The Tarka Trail leaves the Two Moors Way here to go westwards.

Hoaroak Farm (ruin)

Gammons Corner

Hoar Oak Water

HoarOak Tree

ruin

Long Chains Combe Ford

Exe Plain

River Exe

North-bound. Continue north parallel to a fence and through a hunting gate. Turn right to Exe Head through two more gates, then left through the next gate. Follow an old bank till the path reaches a track which swings left into the valley of the Hoar Oak Water. Cross the stream at the foot of Long Chains Combe and follow it northwards to a point opposite the Hoar Oak Tree. Cross the stream again and use the gate in the fence to the left of the tree. Follow the Hoar Oak Water for a further short distance, then cut northwards across open ground onto Cheriton Ridge.

Exe Head

Cairn

TARKA TRAIL

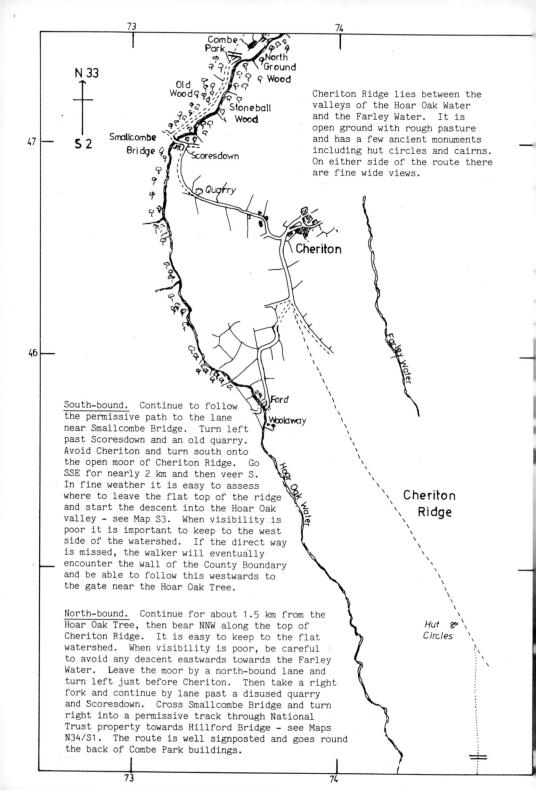

Combe
Park

North
Ground
Wood

Old
Wood

Stoneball
Wood

Smallcombe
Bridge

Scoresdown

N 33

S 2

47

Cheriton Ridge lies between the
valleys of the Hoar Oak Water
and the Farley Water. It is
open ground with rough pasture
and has a few ancient monuments
including hut circles and cairns.
On either side of the route there
are fine wide views.

Quarry

Cheriton

46

Farley water

Cheriton
Ridge

South-bound. Continue to follow
the permissive path to the lane
near Smallcombe Bridge. Turn left
past Scoresdown and an old quarry.
Avoid Cheriton and turn south onto
the open moor of Cheriton Ridge. Go
SSE for nearly 2 km and then veer S.
In fine weather it is easy to assess
where to leave the flat top of the ridge
and start the descent into the Hoar Oak
valley - see Map S3. When visibility is
poor it is important to keep to the west
side of the watershed. If the direct way
is missed, the walker will eventually
encounter the wall of the County Boundary
and be able to follow this westwards to
the gate near the Hoar Oak Tree.

North-bound. Continue for about 1.5 km from the
Hoar Oak Tree, then bear NNW along the top of
Cheriton Ridge. It is easy to keep to the flat
watershed. When visibility is poor, be careful
to avoid any descent eastwards towards the Farley
Water. Leave the moor by a north-bound lane and
turn left just before Cheriton. Then take a right
fork and continue by lane past a disused quarry
and Scoresdown. Cross Smallcombe Bridge and turn
right into a permissive track through National
Trust property towards Hillford Bridge - see Maps
N34/S1. The route is well signposted and goes round
the back of Combe Park buildings.

Ford

Woolaway

Hoar Oak Water

Hut
Circles

South-bound. The Two Moors Way starts opposite the main car park in
Lynmouth. Take the footpath marked 'Watersmeet via the Cleaves', pass
Oxen Tor, where a short cut from Lynbridge Youth Hostel via Summer House
Hill joins the route. Continue past Myrtleberry Hangings to Hillsford.
Use a short stretch of the A 39 before entering National Trust property
at Combe Park Lodge. Follow the permissive path signs, climbing to pass
behind Combe Park.

N 34

S 1

To the seaward side of the path through the Cleaves is
the ravine of the East Lyn River, the precipitous sides
of which plunge about 250 m (800 ft) to the water. The
river so far below looks tiny, but is wider than the
road beside it. The path itself dips steeply to
cross a side stream, but is, in the main,
high with views over the valley to the sea
and to the dry Chisel Combe with Countesbury
Church at its head.

The Hoar Oak Water meets the East Lyn
River a short distance to the east of
the Two Moors Way, which can be left
and rejoined by paths signposted to
'Watersmeet'. The Farley Water joins
the Hoar Oak Water at Hillsford.

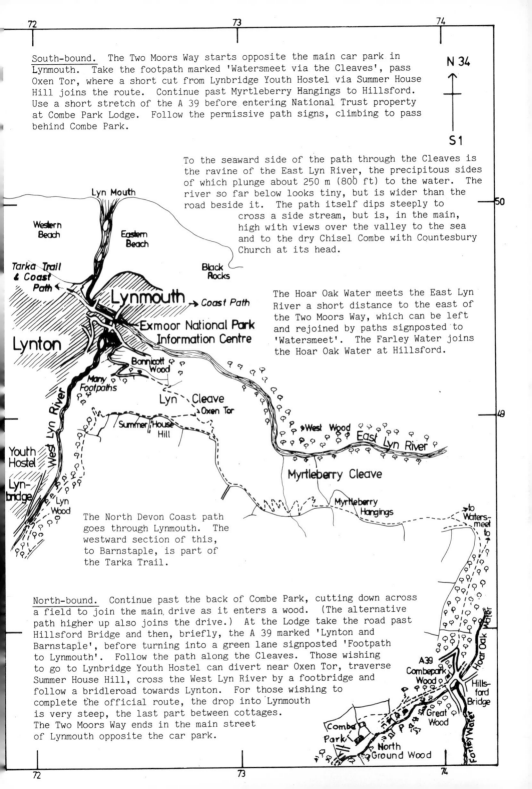

The North Devon Coast path
goes through Lynmouth. The
westward section of this,
to Barnstaple, is part of
the Tarka Trail.

North-bound. Continue past the back of Combe Park, cutting down across
a field to join the main drive as it enters a wood. (The alternative
path higher up also joins the drive.) At the Lodge take the road past
Hillsford Bridge and then, briefly, the A 39 marked 'Lynton and
Barnstaple', before turning into a green lane signposted 'Footpath
to Lynmouth'. Follow the path along the Cleaves. Those wishing
to go to Lynbridge Youth Hostel can divert near Oxen Tor, traverse
Summer House Hill, cross the West Lyn River by a footbridge and
follow a bridleroad towards Lynton. For those wishing to
complete the official route, the drop into Lynmouth
is very steep, the last part between cottages.
The Two Moors Way ends in the main street
of Lynmouth opposite the car park.

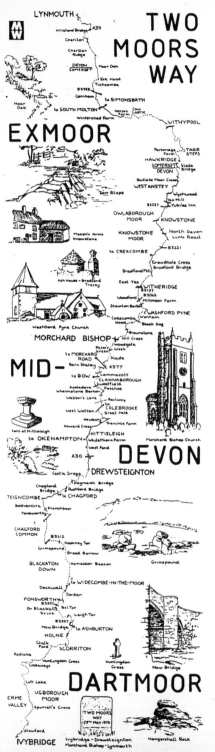

TWO MOORS WAY

EXMOOR

MID-DEVON

DARTMOOR

A Tribute to the work of JOE TURNER

Drawn by Helen Rowett ©1986
Updated and reprinted 1992

ILLUSTRATED MAP OF THE WAY

Black on cream
Actual size 62cm X 21cm
£1.50 + 50p postage & packing

BADGE

White, yellow and black on green
Actual size 6cm X 8.5cm
£1.00 + s.a.e.

ACCOMMODATION

The availability of accommodation
and camping sites near or on the
route of the Two Moors Way changes
from time to time.
Copies of the most recently updated
list can be obtained by sending
s.a.e. plus a 1st class stamp.

All the above items are
available from:-
J.R.Turner,
Coppins,
The Poplars,
Pinhoe,
EXETER. EX4 9HH